The
Thinking
Root

The Thinking Root

THE POETRY OF EARLIEST GREEK PHILOSOPHY

Translated by

Dan Beachy-Quick

MILKWEED EDITIONS

Published 2023 by Milkweed Editions
Printed in the United States of America
Cover design by Mary Austin Speaker
Cover illustration by Mary Austin Speaker
Author photo by Kristy Beachy-Quick
23 24 25 26 27 5 4 3 2 1
First Edition

Library of Congress Cataloging-in-Publication Data

    Names: Beachy-Quick, Dan, 1973- translator.
    Title: The thinking root : the poetry of earliest Greek philosophy /
       [translated by] Dan Beachy-Quick.
    Description: First edition. | Minneapolis, Minnesota : Milkweed Editions,
       2023. | Series: Seedbank | Summary: "From acclaimed poet and translator
       Dan Beachy-Quick comes this new addition to the Seedbank series: a warm,
       vivid translation of the earliest Greek intellects, inviting us to
       reconsider writing, and thinking, as a way of living meaningfully in the
       world"-- Provided by publisher.
    Identifiers: LCCN 2022030325 (print) | LCCN 2022030326 (ebook) | ISBN
       9781571315441 (paperback) | ISBN 9781571317605 (epub)
    Subjects: LCSH: Greek literature--Translations into English.
    Classification: LCC PA3621 .T45 2022 (print) | LCC PA3621 (ebook) | DDC
       881/.0108--dc23/eng/20221206
    LC record available at https://lccn.loc.gov/2022030325
    LC ebook record available at https://lccn.loc.gov/2022030326

Milkweed Editions is committed to ecological stewardship. We strive to align our book production practices with this principle, and to reduce the impact of our operations in the environment. We are a member of the Green Press Initiative, a nonprofit coalition of publishers, manufacturers, and authors working to protect the world's endangered forests and conserve natural resources. *The Thinking Root* was printed on acid-free 100% postconsumer-waste paper by McNaughton & Gunn.

For Hana & Iris—

The baffling hierarchies
Of father and child

As of leaves on their high
Thin twigs to shield us

From time, from open
Time

Contents

Thales, Anaximander, Anaximenes   1
Heraclitus   41
Xenophanes   71
Parmenides, Anaxagoras, Empedocles   79

Sources   129
Acknowledgments   135

"Why should not we also enjoy an original relation to the universe?"

—RALPH WALDO EMERSON, "NATURE"

The
Thinking
Root

Thales, Anaximander, Anaximenes

When we know we do not know, something in us opens. Eyes. Ears. Then we can listen, as Martin Heidegger has it, "to the claim arising out of the thoughtful word." Where we might turn to find a *thoughtful word* is a simple but serious question, as is what a "thoughtful" word might be. I hear in it a word that is full of thought, and more, is full of thought because it is thinking. A word that thinks. It is a subtle difference that shakes our epistemology from bedrock to spire—that inner architecture, that seeming cathedral, the mind. We've thought we think in words, with words, for so long—as if every noun, verb, adjective, article were but a slightly different kind of brick—that we've forgotten a word is its own form of life: one richer, longer, more deeply intelligent than our own. But the builder we might become is the one who puts the brick to ear and listens, who writes the poem not to say anything but to hear what is being said. We might put our inner Daedalus away and learn to live inside the natural labyrinth of the ear, whose intricacy can only be solved by the living thread of the thoughtful word guiding us out and away from the monster we fear—the monster who lives within us, in the center of the maze, and says, "I know, I know." The "claim arising out of the thoughtful word" speaks of existence, the thinking that is existence, introduces us into the fact of being. The rock is a thoughtful word. And so is the cloud, that is only a rock spiritually magnified. So is the rain raining down on the bird that nightlong sings her songs. And who can say where the rock ends and the cloud begins? Who can know the sun doesn't carry darkly in its center a portion of the earth? And the earth and the sun are the same size—that sun I can eclipse with my thumb? We say the night is the opposite of the day, but maybe it's truer to say the night is only the day's thinking carried to its inevitable end; and so the day is also the night's truest thought. Each reveals the other. Day and night are the same. So Thales says of life and death, those opposites. They are the same.

It's easy to confuse the complex with the difficult, but the thoughtful word teaches us to realize the complex isn't difficult at all—it's the simple that's hardest to grasp. Learning to think means learning to walk the path that is thinkable. It is a strange riddle that asks no question. I mean, we must learn to think only about what is there to think about, what reveals itself as itself, what un-conceals itself as something which is true. What is hardest is thinking what is true, which might not feel like thinking at all. It feels like trying to see. Like trying to listen. An experience, not a knowing. A relation, not a mastery. The tremendous, silent fact of the obvious which cannot be denied and which puts us in the thinker's proper position. Not that grief-stricken posture of head resting on hand. But as Heidegger offers it to us: the heedful retreat in the face of being. I picture it as walking backward, eyes fixed on what glows with the full-of-awe inner tension of its finely wrought life, so that what exists can exist all the more. Love and fear, sacred and scared. How can it be that learning to think isn't thinking at all? It's just walking backward along the path you came, undoing the trespass, absorbed in the gaze.

ς

Who are our teachers in such fundamental hopes? Who are the teachers whose lives demonstrate the experiment? They are those who let themselves know less than we know. Who have the bedrock courage not only of not knowing but of being *in* un-knowing. They teach us to dwell thoughtfully in uncertain realms—the realm that is the world, and the realm that is ourselves. The chickadee in the underbrush flits like a thought from branch to branch. The house finch in the blue spruce sings. But there are other teachers, too. The green leaves. And Thales. The shadow beneath the bee and the endless flowers. And Anaximander. The spring morning breeze. And Anaximenes.

We have lost our sense of thinking as the experience that keeps us *in* the world, rather than a theorizing *about* it, but it is such thinking we now need most. The thinking toward thoughtful words that keep us in our heedful retreat. I love that word, "heedful." It is so humble in its attention, so abashed in its faith. So Greek. The tight weave of modern self-consciousness loosens into a questioning fabric, an "I" of the selvage, frayed enough that any breath, any ψυχή, could unravel thread by thread the whole cloth. Which would be fine. Life and death are the same. The opposites pivot around an essential point that cannot be spoken of, though it can be sought; that cannot be seen, though the orbit around the emptiness makes it almost perceptible. The "nothing that is not there and the nothing that is," as Wallace Stevens put it. These thinkers are also each in orbit around essential questions. They ask what we are afraid to ask, or think we are asking, but we aren't. They ask, What are the stars and planets, what the sun and moon, what the earth? How did they come to be, and of what are they made? How the animals? How the human? Why the sea and why then does the ocean pour down from the sky? What the clouds, and what the lightning? What the water? What the air? What the boundless, infinite, unlimited source that births infinite worlds and into which infinite worlds return to die? Who am I who says I?

The questions Thales, Anaximander, and Anaximenes ask are so old, so near the origin of thought that we can no longer ask the questions in the same way, even if we say them in the same words. We think we are seeking knowledge when we ask them; but these philosophers suggest that understanding is something other than knowing the facts—it is the eye's unconscious adjustment to light or dark, the hand's grip around what it holds from which the mind must take its example. The helpless, heedful acceptance of the world as already given. The ancient stays so strangely ahead of us, a thing not yet achieved though once as common as the grass. The hope of this small volume of translations is to offer some experience of what it might be to think as these thinkers thought. To do so means the translation takes an unusual path. Sensing that the standard scholarly presentation that cites the sources in which the texts are found acts mostly as a scaffolding that traces a thinking while also obscuring it, I decided to see what would happen if those attributions were removed, if we had to encounter these words as one might find a broken shard in a field, and then another, and again, knowing somehow they fit together into a vessel entire, but not knowing how to assemble it, not knowing if all the parts have been found, or even if all the shards belong to the same pot. And yet, it almost holds together. And if you could put your hand through the mouth, you might feel the impressions of the fingers that smoothed the coils into a wall solid enough to hold the wine without spilling a drop. Or maybe it was olive oil. Or maybe it was grain. Or maybe the pot is meant to have so many holes, the seeds fall back to the ground. Maybe it's meant to stay broken just enough to let back out what has been poured in—something like that broken pot, the mind.

Each of these translations is organized as I would shape a poem. Image guides and unfolds according to its own inherent logic. This method occasionally prefers poetic accuracy over denotative purity, seeking to tease out the inward possibilities of how certain words might be experienced. Likewise, along with the abandonment of the immediate contextualizing citations typically offer, I free the fragments of their typical groupings, letting the various aspects of their thinking, their biography, and their reception intermingle. In Thales, we move from his immortal sayings to his life to the poem immortalizing him on his gravestone—leaving politics to study among the divine seers in Egypt, his geometric discoveries among the pyramids, and his return to Greece, where he ponders the nature of water, grows rich harvesting olives, and wonders at the nature of the stars. Anaximander's fragments move from outermost cosmos to earth and how life here emerged. For Anaximenes, this thinker in air, I let his own principle be the loose principle of construction: that all comes from a dense thickening undone by rarefaction. Each tries to tell the story of a life and pay heed to the claim a thoughtful life makes—as profound as the claim arising from a "thoughtful word." Of these thinkers of whom only rumors remain, their words caught in writings not their own, these translations humbly hope to let a face gather around the mind, a human face, quick as sparrows, as are our own faces, so quick.

ᔐ

Contradictions abound. As do harmonies. While walking at night looking up at the stars Thales falls down a well. Anaximander, first person to map the land and seas, first to make a globe, theorizes the nature of the cosmos as infinitely without bounds or measure. Anaximenes asks us to understand that all that is comes from oppositional forces acting upon the air: densifying, loosening. According to some, there is a lineage among these thinkers, all located in Miletus, a thriving city on the Maeander River, in what is now modern-day Turkey. Thales, first of all philosophers in the Greek tradition, taught Anaximander who in turn taught Anaximenes. Letting the translations follow one another according to this pedagogical order, one feels how the thin, tensile strings of one man's thought weave themselves into a new mind in the next man. Among the gifts these philosophers bring us is a lesson not only of what it feels like to think but of what it looks like to learn. One such thread: Thales knows the world is one, an infinite one; Anaximander knows that infinite worlds born from a boundless unity die back into their endless source; Anaximenes knows the world can die. Just as we're learning the world can die, Anaximenes already knew it.

Which is to say the simple hope of this book is no more than that the reader can sit down and become a student, too. A student of the obvious. That is, a student of the world revealing itself as world. I'm writing these words with hands made of water and earth, and a mind made mostly of thick air sometimes pierced by a guiding flame. Lethe is the river that flows through my heart. These clouds and rainbows are my eyes. So I've been taught to know myself by translating these thinkers. ("Know thyself," divine utterance Thales first taught.) They remind me to take care of the world. They don't ask me to ask *who* I am. But *what* I am. If I can think it, how can it be far? If I can think it, how can it be hidden, how can it be untrue? I am part of the world; part of the cosmos. And so are you.

THALES
—for Srikanth Reddy

... and according to some, he left behind no writing ...

And among his everlasting songs are these:

> Not one of the many words reveals a thought
> right-minded ...

> Wisdom is in seeking one thing ...

> Let the mind grasp the one thing it cherishes ...

> You will, like the ox unbound from the yoke, loosen
> tongues from the endless babble of men

The first Greeks philosophizing about the heavenly stars and divine powers ... such as Thales, all agree and say the same ... wrote very little. And these writings for the Greeks seem of all things most ancient, and they can barely believe them having been written at all.

And these apothegms are attributed to him:

The oldest of beings is a god; the gods were never born.

The cosmos is order most beautiful—a poem written by
a god.

The field entire is what is largest, its acres open to all.

The mind is what is quickest, running swift through
everything.

Necessity is what is most strong; necessity conquers all.

Wisest is time, for time finds out all things.

The divine utterance "Know thyself" is Thales's own, so says
Antisthenes in *The Successions*, though Chilon claims the phrase
for himself.

After studying politics, he became one who watches the world,
theorizer of the pure orders, and, some say, was the first to speak
about nature.

No one explained the way for him, except that setting out to
Egypt, he spent time together with the holy priests.

. . . Pythagoras urged him to sail to Egypt and, in Memphis and Diospolis, to sojourn with the best of the divine seers; for it was among them he was given these things he knows and learned the practices for which many people think him wise.

From the Egyptians he learned to measure geometrically, says Pamphile, first drew a right triangle within a circle, and (in thanks) sacrificed, as burnt offering, an ox. Others, like Apollodorus the logician, claim for Pythagoras the honor.

Thales believes the Etesian winds that blow against Egypt lift up the Nile's flowing bulk because its outflowing waters are opposed by the swelling open sea driven back against it.

And all things are borne along and flow, giving birth to themselves, the world weaving itself whole, according to the first cause. This is a god: the never-beginning-never-ending one.

You stuck your walking stick at the edge of the shadow the pyramid cast, and as the touch of the sunray made two triangles, you showed the ratio that shadow to shadow holds is the same ratio as pyramid to staff.

This theory brought to light that when two straight lines cut through each other, the angles formed are equal; a discovery, says Eudemos, made first by Thales.

Hieronomos also says he measured the pyramids by their shadows, watching closely for when our shadows equal ourselves.

Eudemos, in *The History of Geometry*, says that Thales brought to light this theory. He says it is a way to reveal the distance of ships at sea, which, they say, is necessary to use.

It is through ancient Thales, who among many other discoveries, found this beautiful theory. They say he was first to understand and to claim that the base angles of all isosceles triangles are equal, though in his antique manner he said "similar seeming" for "equal."

They say Thales was first to show that a circle is cut in two by its diameter . . .

He was first to find the path by which season turned to season, and according to some, was first to declare the sun's magnitude and the moon's size—the 720th part of the solar and lunar circles.

Of the seasons of the year they say he discovered they divide into 365 days.

Followers of Thales say the earth is in the middle ...

... from earth is the sun.

... the sun throws light on the moon.

Eudemos records in *The Astrologies* that Thales revealed the sun's eclipse and discovered, of the sun's turning along its yearly cycle, that its period is not always equal.

Thales first said the sun's eclipse is caused by the moon—moon whose matter is made of earth—moving directly underneath it, as one sees when a disk drops down on a mirror.

After he philosophized in Egypt, he came back to Miletus an old man.

The historian Heraclides said that Thales remained alone and belonged only to himself. But some say he married and had a son named Cybisthus; others say he stayed unmarried but brought his sister's son into his home.

To someone seeking to learn which came first, night or day, "The night," he said, "came first by a day."

When asked why he had no child, he answered, "Because of my love for children." And they say that when his mother tried to guilt him into marrying, he said, "The time has not yet come." Then, when old age had wrapped itself like a cloak around him, he said, "Time is no longer."

"The same gifts you brought your parents," he says, "your children will bring to you."

Before us or far away, he says we should remember those we love: "Not for their beautiful faces but for the beauty they bring to the world, which is the beauty they are."

. . . all things are full of gods.

When Croesus came to the river Halys, thereupon—just as I say—the army crossed on bridges already built, but according to a story among many of the Greeks, Thales of Miletus got them across. When Croesus didn't understand how to get his army across the river (these bridges not yet built at this time), they say that Thales, who was in the camp, made the river, which flowed on the left-hand side of the army, to flow on the right-hand side as well. He began by digging a deep, crescent-shaped trench above the camp, like the shape of the sun in partial eclipse; turned aside by the trench, the water coursed behind the camp, diverted from its original bed, so that, split where the river ran swiftest, both streams became fordable.

Someone asked what is difficult; he said, "To know oneself." What is easiest? "To give advice to someone else." What is happiness? "To do what you say you'll do." What is divine? "That which has no beginning and has no end." What thing has he never seen? He said, "A tyrant grown old."

He also seems to have offered to citizens the best advice. When Croesus sent men to Miletus to form an alliance, he hindered it; this saved the city after Cyrus conquered.

When the same war raged inconclusively for years, during a battle in the sixth year, day suddenly became night. Thales of Miletus told the Ionians this change would occur, by knowing the heavens knowing beforehand the year the eclipse would come.

Timon knows him also as an astronomer, and in his *Lampoons* praises him, saying:

> Thales, wise alone among the seven sages,
> Studied the stars . . .

Callimachus thought Thales discovered the Little Bear, saying in his *Iambs*:

> And he was said to have measured the framework
> Of the little stars, by which the Phoenicians sailed at
>   night the sea

. . . of astronomy written by him, Lobon of Argos says, he left behind two hundred lines . . .

. . . the stars are earthlike embers burning in ash.

And Thales, studying the stars, looking up past sight's end, fell down into a well; a smart, graceful Thracian serving girl chiding said, "You're so eager to know the heavens, you don't see what's in front of your feet."

Scolding him for his poverty, the people said philosophy had no use. But by observing the stars, it is said, and though it was still winter, he learned the crop of olives would be abundant. He put the few dollars he had down as earnest payment on all the olive presses in Miletus and Chios, renting them cheaply, for no one was competing against him. When time came ripe, many men all at once suddenly searched him out, and he rented out turns on the presses to whomever he wished. By carrying away so much money he showed how easy it is for philosophers to be wealthy if they wished, but money is not what they study.

. . . the cosmos is the mind of a god, and all that breathes is full of divinities; holy thought reaches through and lifts up the whirling water, putting itself in motion.

"Don't get rich," he says, "by evil means; and don't let a word spoken break the trust you share in others."

As if the words spoken about the earth didn't also speak of the water the earth bears.

... that Thales declared the only element to be water, from his writing itself we cannot offer proof, though everyone believes this true.

He said that everything begins and ends in water. From it all things come together, take root, and fall back apart; all things rest upon it; and it is water that shakes the earth, whirls together the winds, and sets the stars in their shining dance.

Thales also says that all that lives comes from water, but he also wanted to say something more strongly; and to find the expression, turn to the second book of *On the Elements*, which offers it in this way: "Of the four known by so many, the first is water, and though they speak of it as if it were the only element, the four combine and fit solidly and closely together, commingling all the things of the daily world. How this happens we already spoke of in Volume 1."

Nevertheless, not all the philosophers say the same thing of the number and form of these original elements, though Thales claims water to be first (and so declared the earth floats on water) ...

Maybe he grasped this notion from seeing that all things are nourished by moisture, and heat itself forms from water, and so all life lives (and of all which comes into being, this is life's source)—so he kept hold of his idea, also because the seeds of all things have a moist nature; for water is the cause of things naturally moist. But there are some men who, in ancient times, long before generations now born first spoke of the logic of the gods, also understood this thought about nature: they made Oceanus and Tethys parents of what rose into unfolding being, made water the object of the gods' own oaths, called Styx by the poets—river worshipped most and most ancient, and an oath itself the thing most honored. If this hand-built thought can be gripped, and water is truly nature's ancient cause, this idea won't be lost to our sight; but people claim Thales brought to light this first cause.

Some say the soul is mixed in with the whole world, from which Thales thought all things are full of gods.

Some people say he was first to claim the soul is deathless . . .

Thales first revealed the soul's nature: eternally self-moving.

... the cosmos is a corpse that breathes and is full of divinities.

... the world is one.

Aristotle and Hippias say that he believed even lifeless things have their share of soul, pointing out the magnetic stone and electrum.

So the wise man came to his end sitting at the athletic contests, thirsty and weak in the scorching heat, having reached an old age.

"Death," he said, "is no different than life." "If so," someone said, "why don't you die?" "Because there is no difference," he said.

His statue bears this inscription:

This is Thales of Miletus, nourished and raised in Ionia,
    Of all who study the logic of the stars, most honored,
        most wise.

ANAXIMANDER

—*for Mai Wagner*

Anaximander of Miletus, son of Praxiades . . .

Anaximander, friend of Thales, and fellow citizen . . .

Anaximander of Miletus, son of Praxiades, whose mind Thales
birthed, his student and his successor . . .

Diodorus of Ephesus, writing about Anaximander, says that he
affected a tragic pomp (like a goatskin swollen with wine) and
donned clothes to look like a holy man.

Eratosthenes says, and Hecataeus of Miletus agrees, that
Homer and Anaximander were the first two to publish books
on geography.

. . . among the Greeks of whom we know, he was the first to
bring forth, from hard toil, a book on the nature of Nature.

Like a child left waiting in a field, he wrote down a summary of his principal thoughts, which somehow Apollodorus of Athens happened to find.

He wrote *On Nature, The Wandering Earth, Of the Constant Stars, Sphere,* and one other book.

ऽ

. . . the unbound heavens are gods.

. . . out from the confusion of heat and cold.

. . . infinite worlds enfolded in the infinite.

. . . the world is full of ruin.

He was first to suggest boundlessness, holding it necessary to have something endlessly bounteous for these endless birthings; and worlds are boundless, and each world is of this element that is this boundlessness; so he thought.

And yet it is also formless and everlasting, uncreated and undecaying, the one cause of the world. For what comes to be, Necessity fates to an end; and the end of all things is ruin. This is why, exactly as we're saying, this originating principle has no cause, but itself seems to be the cause of others, cycling through everything and steering all, as those others say, who argue for no other cause than the boundless . . . and this boundlessness is god.

Philosophers who claim infinite worlds move throughout the infinite, as does Anaximander, say those worlds are born and destroyed forever, some unfolding into being, others falling to ruin, and they say, like an endless elegy, the motion is eternal— minus this motion there is no life or death.

Anaximander says that the source of being is boundless: out from it all comes to be and into it all falls to ruin. For it is from this boundlessness that the infinite cosmos is born, and to this boundlessness it returns, destroyed by what it emerged from. At least he says this boundlessness is why nothing is lacking from the genesis of the world coming to be . . .

The other thinkers in singular elements say that the One contains oppositions that grow separate from it, just as Anaximander says, and all those others who say the One and the Many exist, such as Empedocles and Anaxagoras—for they also think all other things separate out from this mixed unity.

Of the philosophers who declare there are infinite worlds, Anaximander says they are kept separate by the same distance.

The philosophers of nature speak in two ways. There are those who consider the body as established and lying underneath, one of three elements or some other, denser than fire and thinner than air, bringing the myriad into being by condensing and rarifying.... The others say all things have substance in the One and are expelled out from it, just as Anaximander says ...

All those men studying physics put the boundless under certain other natures called elements, like water or air or a mixture of these.

It was clear to him, his wondrous gaze seeing the four elements change one into another, that he did not think one should be the foundation of all things, but some other thing besides.

Anaximander spoke of an element as something indiscernible—finer than air, denser than water—since the underlying foundation must be well suited to transform into both air and water.

. . . the fundamental element is the boundless, not the determinate air, not water, and not any other. Portions may change, but the whole is unalterable.

Some thinkers assumed as primary one element—some water, some air, some fire, some something finer than water and denser than air—but Anaximander says the boundless surrounds the heavens entire.

. . . the sun's circle is nineteen times larger than the earth's, and the sun is just like a chariot wheel, hollow rim full of fire, tilted over, flame breathing out as through the holes drilled in a flute, an eclipse at the turning of the wheel.

. . . it is twenty-eight times the size of the earth, is like a chariot's wheel with a curving, hollow rim full of fire, and one part flames out as fire would through the holes drilled in a flute—and this is the sun.

. . . when the mouth that breathes out fire closes, an eclipse.

. . . the sun is equal to the earth, but its circle, through which its fire breathes out and by which it moves across the sky, is twenty-seven times larger than the earth.

. . . the moon has its own, somehow thinner, light.

. . . the earth is high aloft in the air, resting in the middle of the universe.

In the middle rests the earth, a bubble balanced on a spear's sharp point.

Some say its likeness keeps the earth lodged in place, as among the ancients, Anaximander. For it holds that the earth that sits still in equal relation to the extremities should never move up or down or to the side; and it is impossible to move in opposite directions at the same time. Necessity says that the earth stands still.

... the earth is like a never-crumbling column of stone.

... the air, dense as wool pressed into felt, is a wheel, like a pot-ter's wheel, full of fire, and one portion blazes out, like breath from out a mouth.

... the wind is a flow of air, air itself being but the finest par-ticles of moisture, that the sun sets in motion and melts down into rain.

Anaximander links the nature of the soul to air.

Aristotle included in his history the opinion of Anaximander, who posited as a principle of nature a mixture of air and fire, or of air and water—it is said in both ways.

... the seas are relict of the original moisture, the largest waters fire dried up, the remainder transformed by the kindling heat.

At first the earthly realm was thoroughly sodden, but the sun dried it; that vapor formed the breathing winds that turn and return their essence to the sun and moon; what moisture remained created the seas—and so they think it grows smaller as it dries, and one day the entire ocean will evaporate completely.

These thinkers say the sea is born, unlike the theologians, who say the sea had no birth but has a source running ever into itself. Some men say the sea is but a remnant of the first moisture. Wet was the region around the earth, and the sun evaporated some portion of the moisture, creating the winds that turn, and the turning of the seasons, the turning of the sun and the moon, for these vapors' rising exhalations cause these turnings. The sun and moon return to the place of these influencing vapors. The moisture left behind in the hollows of the earth are the oceans— eventually, the sun will parch the oceans, diminish the waters, and the earth will be dry. These are the opinions, as Theophrastus tells, held by Anaximander and Diogenes.

. . . lightning storm and thunder, tornado and cyclone, even the slight drizzle of rain, even the shroud of mist, these all come from the breathing influence of the wind. A thick cloud embraces all these, but, as if a fist fell down and shattered it, it breaks apart, so fine and light are the particles of which it's made; a burst of noise cracks the dark cloud open and ends in lightning's bright splendor leaping out.

After Thales, Anaximander . . . revealed the unbound-limitless-infinite is the whole cause of all that is born and falls to ruin, and he also says that from this boundlessness the heavens, like long hair, are shorn, as are all the countless worlds. He declared that destruction arrived, as much earlier came birth, from the infinite, ever-living, ever-turning, and ever-returning whole. He says the shape of the earth is cylindrical, its height one third of its width. He says at the beginning this world was separated from the fertile heat and everlasting cold, and a fire-bright sphere, smooth like the bark of the olive tree, grew around the air that encircles the earth. When this broke apart, the tatters closed and formed into other circles—the sun, the moon, and the stars. He says that originally humans emerged from other animals of different forms, each of which gestates swiftly, but humans alone need to be nursed a long time—which is why, being such creatures, we could not survive the world's beginning.

. . . from the ur-dew the first animals emerged, surrounded by a thin, thorny husk; but growing in age, they moved to drier places, the bark burst open, and, in a little time, their way of living changed.

He did not think that fish and humans each came in and of themselves, but revealed that first humans were born and grew within fish, like dogfish or sharks, and when they'd grown enough to take care of themselves, they emerged, stepping out onto the earth.

Those descended from the ancient Greeks burn sacrifices to ancestral Poseidon, thinking that humans emerged out of the original moisture, just as the Syrians also think—which is why they hold the fish sacred, born together and reared together, as philosophers more reasonable than Anaximander theorized. And just as fire devours the wood that is its mother and father both, Anaximander laid blame against those who eat fish, which share our common parentage.

This principle, he said, is that beings have some infinite nature, from which the heavens form and the worldly orders within them. It is everlasting and never decays, and engulfs all the cosmos. He speaks of time as source of immediate reality and its destruction. The primary elements of being, he said, are boundless, and this term he was first to call a principle. Their motion is eternal dance, and they come together to form the heavens. The earth is risen up aloft, ruled by nothing, staying still because it is at an equal distance from all things. Its form is fluid, rounded, looking like a column of stone; of its surfaces, one is the ground we're stepping on, the other is the opposite ground we can't step on. The stars are circles of fire, set apart from the cosmic flame. There are vents, like certain holes in a musical pipe, through which the stars appear—and when these are stopped up, as a finger presses down to play a note, an eclipse comes to be. When the moon appears full, and when it lessens, it is by the holes closing or opening. The circle of the sun is twenty-seven times the size of the moon; and the sun holds the highest position, the fixed stars the lowest. The life of animals is drawn up as a vapor from the sun. Humans came to be as another animal did—the fish—which in the beginning were nearly the same. The winds come to be by thinnest separation from the vapors of the air and, gathering their motions together, blow; rain comes from the vapors of the earth that the sun draws up; lightning, when the wind crashes down and blows apart the clouds.

＄

This man first built the gnomon to discern the solstices of the sun, time and the seasons' hours, and the equinoxes.

He discovered first the gnomon and stood it up on the sundials in Sparta, so says Favorinus in his *Miscellaneous History*, showing by a sign the turn of the solstice and the equinox, and constructing the horoscope.

It is said that the children ridiculed his singing, and learning of which, he said: "Then for the good of the children, I must learn to sing better."

ANAXIMENES

—*for Martin Corless-Smith*

He used to speak in an Ionic style, simple and plain.

... the sun is a flat leaf.

... the circling outermost from the earth is the heavens.

... like nails struck the stars are stuck, crystalline in the sky

   ... &

... some say, as on a painting, the stars are fiery leaves.

... the moon holds the sun's light ...

... fiery indeed is the nature of the stars, but they contain some
earthly body they carry invisibly around within them.

Anaximenes and Diogenes place air before water as the better principle among the simplest bodies . . .

Anaximenes, just as Anaximander did, thought nature under-girded by something singular and infinite, but, unlike his teacher, did not think it indefinite and undetermined but certain—he said it is the air. It alters from thinnest (as of a cloth loosely woven) to most dense depending on its substance—when thin it becomes fire; when denser it is wind; then cloud building on cloud; then, denser yet, water; then loose earth; then stone. All else comes from these. This motion he considered eternal, and all change comes through it.

. . . air is revealed as the principle of being—all emerges from air and into air dissolves. "Just as our soul," he says, "is the air that holds us together, the cosmos entire is embraced by breath and air." He spoke as if air and breath were synonyms.

It is necessary, to hear what these men are saying of the air as a god, to listen as a student listens and learn, of elements and bodies, their dynamic force.

They say Anaximenes spoke of air as the fundamental rule of the universe, and that air is of the same nature as the boundless, and about this thought he was sure of himself, that all things come to be from some dense gathering of air that later loosens. This motion reaches through time's eternal span—a contraction of the air, he says, gave birth to the earth, which was very flat, like the blade of an oar or wing. So logic says the earth rides upon the air. The sun, the moon, and the stars are descendants of the earth, genesis of the same rule. At the very least, he shows that the sun is of the earth, and like a thrown spear, crosses the sky.

The ancient astrologers persuaded many that the sun does not move under the earth but in the region around it, hides away to make the night by rising to the north, high above the earth.

. . . a trapezium, shaped like a table

. . . &

. . . by its flatness it floats on the air.

. . . flatness of the earth causes it to stay still. It does not cut but covers like a lid the air below it, as flat bodies are seen to do— it's hard for the winds, too, to move them, these bodies so resistant to the force of the gust. He says the earth in its flatness acts the same on the air lying under it (and there being no room for the air to move, it remains fixed, a dense mass below the earth), just like water in the water clock. And that the air can receive and bear great weight and remain motionless, speaks many proofs.

The one principle of all beings, boundlessness set in motion, is, in the opinion of Anaximenes, the air. He says: "The air is nearly bodiless, and by its flowing out we come to be, a source in itself endlessly abundant, that never empties, never closes.

... the principle element is boundless air, and all that is, all that was, all that will be, even the gods and the deathless divinities, are children born of the air. The idea of the air is this: it is wholly equal to itself, invisible to the eye, but its motions can be seen in cold, in heat, and in moisture. Its motion is eternal: for what turns so suddenly around could not, if there were no movement. It reveals itself differently when thick or of looser weave—loose and spread out, kindles *fire*; *wind* is the ancient air thickening; the air compressed brings the wool of *clouds*; then *water*; denser yet, *earth*; and the densest is *stone*. The lords of generation are opposites: heat and cold.

The earth is a thin wing riding on the air; similarly, the sun, the moon, the stars, and all the fiery others settle their thin selves on the air. The heavenly bodies emerge from the earth, rising with the moisture, like sleepers roused from sleep. From rarefication, fire lights up; and from this fire rising to a height, the stars are arranged in their order. There is something earthly in the nature of the stars and planets, traveling with them in their turnings. He says the stars do not move below the earth, as others thought, but around it, just as is the case with a felt cap worn close-fitting around the head. The sun hidden not because it is below the earth but because it takes refuge so far above it, at so great a distance from us. And the stars, so distant, give off no heat.

The winds arise when dense air loosens and is borne away; and the winds coming together, growing thick in strength, create the clouds, and from these clouds the rain falls. Hail hails down when the falling rain freezes; snow snows when these same drops, grown more watery, freeze, crystalline. When the clouds, by their own wild winds, blow themselves apart: lightning— bright, bifurcating bolts of fire. When the sun's beams fall down on the gathered air: a rainbow. The earth in earthquake shakes when greatly transformed by heat and cold.

Anaximenes wants to think that moisture and air create the wind, which flows with some unknown force, crossing the sky as swiftly as winging birds.

He says the drawing close together and growing dense is cold-ness, and (by the names he used himself) air loosening and growing slack is heat. Not unreasonably, he says that a man breathes out heat and cold from his mouth: breathing hard, lips pressed close, breath thickens and is cooled; relaxed and open, out the mouth falls heat, the breath loosened . . .

. . . clouds grow fat when the air is under great pressure, and when more pressure begins to gather, the rainstorm is pressed out from the clouds; snow when water falling freezes; hail when wind embraces moisture.

. . . the rainbow comes to be by the radiance of the sun on dense, thick, dark clouds—since the bright beams cannot cut the cloud in two, the light gathers into itself.

. . . a rainbow appears when the sun's rays fall down on air dense and thick. First from the sun purple appears, burnt through by bright beams, then dark, overmastered by moisture. And at night the moon makes the rainbow, though not often, the moon not always full, and its light weaker than the sun's.

. . . not one of these things is caused by any of those but by the sun alone.

Of meteorological phenomena, Anaximenes agrees with his teacher, Anaximander, adding this about the sea: that struck by an oar the water gleams.

᠘

Anaximenes says that drenching and drying shatters the earth, and from this shaking, the hills break apart and fall down—and so, in times of drought and floods of heavy rains, earthquakes also come. For in drought, as has been said, the dry earth cracks, and when too much moisture soaks in, it crumbles apart.

The world is made to be born and to die; though some say the world is eternal, it is not always the same, but periodically comes into being and at other times perishes, just as Anaximenes says.

... dense air struck a mighty blow and out tossed the stars.

... countless worlds by boundlessness surrounded.

... the world can die.

... the soul is like air.

... the air ...

Heraclitus

Most of what is known isn't known. Rumor labors across centuries to dismantle the scaffolding of facts. What is revealed is truer than the truth, an inheritance beyond death's reach. It comes not as a gold coin to save against future oblivion or a golden thread within history's whole weaving—it comes like wind blown through an olive tree, scent unfolding the orchard behind the eyes. It is a bewildering education, and one far from complete, to learn how to listen to those rare voices who live in that orchard and nowhere else, whose toil is to harvest those thoughts that grow best beneath the mind, not in it. At such depths a syllable is an epistemology; so is a single olive; so is a single seed. A strange inward listening might teach us all we can know, a kind of eavesdropping on the heroes of old who dwell in the undergrove, gossiping among themselves to pass the endless hours. What we learn does not feel like knowledge. It feels like the want to know, the desire that precedes knowledge and pursues it, as a child pursues the names of nameless things.

One of those heroes, Heraclitus, says, "I sought myself." It can be translated in other ways. *I searched myself. I searched for myself. I searched through myself.* What each translation reveals isn't a fact but a thoughtful suspicion. Like nature, the self loves to hide. It hides in itself; or, to learn the lesson more honestly, I hide in myself, or my self hides in me. What should be unquestionably present has wandered off—not to a distance but to a depth. This first philosophic work asks us to ask ourselves who all it is that lives within us, lets us understand that an inward turn can be self-searching rather than self-involved. What do we find? I'd like to think we find ourselves in the orchard among those thinkers dearest to us, breath scented with the olives just picked. It would mean that we must learn to do as Odysseus did and carry ourselves into death and gather what advice we can. It would mean that we are ourselves the underworld we must enter. That isn't psychology in the current sense; it is *psuch*ology in the ancient sense. The logic of the *soul* that is the logic of the *breath* that is the logic of the *butterfly* that is a symbol of death and death's transformation. Heraclitus knows life and death aren't opposites: "The deathless are the dying, the dying are the deathless—one is living the other's death, one is dying into the other's life." The paradox might reveal that we are also among the dead who live within us, learning to listen so that, when night comes on, and we hear Heraclitus saying, "death is what wakes us and calls us forth, and sleep is what puts us to rest," we might seek that path back out of ourselves, reciting what we've come to know, remembering not to look back, and to live our daylit lives wakeful as we can manage to be.

§

Heraclitus deposited the book for which he is renowned in the temple of Artemis in Ephesus. It is to this same temple he would retreat to play at knucklebones with boys, and when found there by the city's leaders, Heraclitus scorned them: "Why, you rascals, are you astonished? Is it not better to do this than to take part in your civil life?" Embedded obscurely in the jibe lurks an aspect of his philosophy. Dubious of those "laws" civilized men legislate to create social order, Heraclitus saw in playing with boys a game of chance revelation of a cosmic order. Far from profaning the holy precinct, tossing the knucklebones and—depending on the side on which they landed—tallying up the points allowed some force beyond the human to dictate the outcome of the hand's throw. The child's game traces the lines of Fate and Chance, and to accept the results is to surrender oneself to the deeper Laws by which the world works. The games of children reveal the foundational orders of the world, which, in the depth of their necessity, mock the rules men build to convince themselves of their authority. True laws cannot be seen—they are obscure; they also love to hide. But our lives limn the possibilities available to us, near the Fact as the asymptote nears the axis, not as an aspect of will but of surrender to the strange and ever-opening realization that one exists. Heraclitus might remind us that it is not for us to describe life; we are ourselves life's description. We must learn to read ourselves, curious primer to the world. Of the goddess guarding Heraclitus's book, or the goddess to whom the book is offered, we might note as Martin Heidegger does that she carries in one hand a bow or a lyre and in the other a torch. The bow and the lyre both work along the same principle of harmony, one Heraclitus thinks much about, in which the concept eclipses the musical and encroaches on the metaphysical, where harmony is a jointure, a point of contradiction, as the arrow is flung by the string that in being drawn back draws together the extremes of the wood, as the musical note is flung out by the same process. Both arrow and music bring some aspect of death—the arrow's barb, the note's eternity. Her other hand bears the torch, giver of light, symbol of life, sign of what reason can know. Artemis is a goddess of pure paradox, bringer of life and death, bearer of day and night. She is the divine embodiment of Heraclitus's thought, the holy proof of his overriding sense that contradiction isn't a failure in logic but the means to move past it and realize, as he does, that *all is one.*

Let his response to the Ephesian noblemen stand for the philosopher's general disposition toward people. He became a misanthrope, a hater of humankind. He wandered from the city to live in the hills, living as wild creatures live, on seeds, herbs, and grasses. Despite himself he became famous, all the more so for the difficulty the writing presented. Followers named themselves after him. Euripides brought a copy to Socrates. The Persian king Darius wrote to the philosopher in admiration of the challenges the text presented: "You are the author of the treatise *On Nature* which is hard to understand and hard to interpret. In certain parts, if it be interpreted word for word, it seems to contain a power of speculation on the whole universe and all that goes on within it, which depends upon motion most divine; but for the most part judgment is suspended, so that even those who are the most conversant with literature are at a loss to know what is the right interpretation of your work." King Darius invites him to his palace to have daily conversations, promising every luxury the royal court holds. Heraclitus responded: "All men upon earth hold aloof from truth and justice, while, by reason of wicked folly, they devote themselves to avarice and thirst for popularity. But I, being forgetful of all wickedness, shunning the general satiety which is closely joined with envy, and because I have a horror of splendor, could not come to Persia, being content with little, when that little is my mind."

The little content that is the mind is also a form of the universal all, and the flux of the eternal orders flows through the nervy circuits just as does the blood. The splendors of the palace in all their gilt brightness would only dim the eyes to those bowls filled with fire: the stars. Wickedness is no more than thinking oneself other than or beyond the stuff of the world. Justice, like the lyre's cord, like the bow's string, resonates so that some taut thread sings in us at the same pitch. The question is: how learn to listen? Heraclitus: "Wisdom is in listening." What one listens to is *logos*. Logos is a word of profound inner complications, a tangle of nervous energies, a knot of universal simultaneities. It means, in part, *computation-account-reckoning-measure-consideration-tale-estimation-relation-reason-ratio-proportion-theory-statement-proposition-plea-principle-law-thesis-debate-thinking-creative reason-fable-legend-logic-speech-rumor-divine utterance-common gossip-sentence-word or wisdom-of-gods*, and, most anciently, via the related verb *legein, harvesting, gathering*. What all it is our words gather when words gather in us. Heraclitus: "Of this word that always is, men are fools and can't grasp it; not when they hear it the first time; not when listening with their whole lives ahead of them. Men seem ignorant of it, though all things come to be through this Logos; and when they try to understand and work through the sorts of things I describe, they break apart each word down to its core and try to point out what's really there. As asleep you forget who you are and what you've done, most men walk through their days as if they forgot to wake up." But, Heraclitus knows, even the sleepers are at work bringing forth the world. Of this Logos that always is and is nowhere found, none can arrive and none can hide away.

To claim that paradox is the central figure in Heraclitus's thought is an impoverished turn to literary trope where only experience comes to proper account. The glib say, "I don't know," and it sounds just the same as the truly bewildered. We might recall that in ancient Greek, the word *ethos* speaks to the way one is in the place that is oneself. The mind cleaves in two, and in the crack a voice speaks. It says, "The sun is new each day." It says, "Were there no sun, other stars would still kindle kind night." It says, as Sir Thomas Browne does, channeling across the millennia something of Heraclitean wisdom, "Life is a pure flame, and we live by an invisible sun within us." Heraclitus reminds us, as we must be reminded, for we are no good at saying so to ourselves, that the work isn't to learn *what* to think but *how* to think. The work is getting back to the beginning, and, wondrously, fearfully, like every utmost horizon, the beginning has no end at all.

⸲

But Heraclitus had an end. His meager diet gave him dropsy, and his body swelled with the excess water it could not shed. Irony imbibes such liquid. In many fragments, Heraclitus speaks of the soul's delight in getting wet, but how that moisture is its death, that a dry soul, a soul of dry heat, is best. Dying himself of such moisture, Heraclitus left the hills and came to town to see a doctor and ask how his intestines might be rid of the water they held. Being told there was no remedy, he plastered himself with cow dung and lay down beneath the bright sun, hoping the water would be drawn out of his body. The cure didn't work. He died at the age of sixty. Some say he was buried in the marketplace. Others, that, because he was unable to tear off the dung coating him, that dogs came and devoured him, a cynical thought where no remains remain. Just the fragments.

One of those fragments is a story. Drawn by his renown as a great thinker, some visitors sought Heraclitus in his home. Finding the hovel high in the hills, they stood at the doorway peering in, seeing not a philosopher at his studies but a man warming his feet by a fire. Disappointed or confused by the homely picture, the men did not enter and did not leave, just lingered uncomfortably at the threshold. To end their hesitation, Heraclitus called out, "Even here are the gods."

This humble story might capture Heraclitus's true greatness. He believed that all things come from fire and to fire return, that the good order of the world is of fire everlasting, that fire judges and condemns everything it approaches, that lightning (fire condensed) steers all. Heraclitus also knows the fire burning in his home is that same fire, and the acts of true devotion are the humble cares of our daily lives: baking the oats into poor bread, warming our feet by the same fire. Heraclitus sees, and so asks us to see, that the world is full of gods, and life the sacred work of being among them. The sacred rites don't belong in the temples alone; they may not belong in the temples at all, where people are fooled by the sense of their own holiness. That the fundamental force that is fire humbles itself to burn in a hearth and just there kindly glows offers a small glimpse of our true position among the primary powers. We are among them. The least gesture initiates us into the mysteries. Washing our hands and face. Falling asleep. Waking up. Kindling a fire. Its heat warms the rooms we live in. The same fire keeps the soul sane. The sun itself is a flame burning at the end of a twig.

FRAGMENTS

—*for Del Harrow*

To say as I say isn't wisdom; wisdom is listening to the words, and all words are one.

Of this *word* that always *is*, men are fools and can't grasp it; not when they hear it the first time; not when listening with their whole lives ahead of them. Men seem ignorant of it, though all things come to be through this *logos*; and when they try to understand and work through the sorts of things I describe, they break apart each word down to its core and try to point out what's really there. As asleep you forget who you are and what you've done, most men walk through their days as if they forgot to wake up.

When fools listen, they are like the deaf; a voice from heaven itself says so: a fool arrives already departed.

Eyes and ears give bad witness to men and savage their souls.

Most men don't know how to think about what they face, and they don't know what they've studied; they act as if they understand; they seem to think they know absolutely themselves.

They listen not understanding what to do or what to say.

Without hope you don't find that thing beyond hope which hides and can't be held.

Diggers dig up much earth to find a little gold.

Near the open question.

Nature loves to hide.

Nature loves to play hide and seek among the graves.

The lord who is oracle in Delphi does not speak clearly or hide away; he shows a sign.

The sibyl with madness raging in her mouth reveals what cannot be laughed away, bleats out bare, bitter syllables, arrives (as a suppliant does) at a thousand truths, all through the voice of a god.

What can be known by looking and listening I honor most.

Now is the true time, when everywhere can—by sea or by crossing land—be reached, and we need no poets or mythmakers to explain what can't be understood, as most men who came before us did; to not trust men who set themselves apart by offering certainties; so offers Heraclitus.

Eyes bear witness more accurately than ears.

Much study doesn't teach the mind to hold what it learns; otherwise Hesiod would have had understanding, and also Pythagoras, Xenophon, and Hecataeus.

Pythagoras, son of Mnesarchus, more than all other men, researched curiously his questions, and writing these things down, considered them his own; wisdom much-studied is a fraudulent art.

Of those to whose words I've listened, not one comes near this truth: to know that wisdom is separate from all things.

Wisdom is one—to feel sure of the thought that steers all things through everything.

Neither gods nor men made this world's all-things-in-good-order, but it always was and always is fire everlasting, in measure kindled to flame, in measure burning out.

Fire changes first to sea; and the sea is half earth, and half swollen storm laced with lightning.

All things return to fire and fire returns to all things, as gold becomes goods and goods become gold.

Diffused in the sea and measured out by the same logic as before it was and came to be.

Want . . . satiety.

Fire's life is the death of air, air's life is the death of fire; water's life is the death of earth, earth's of water.

Fire judges and condemns all things it approaches.

From what never departs who can hide away?

A thunderbolt holds the reins.

The sun will not overstep his measure; and, if he does, Justice's mercenaries, the Furies themselves, will hunt him down.

The turning post of morning and evening is the Bear, and opposite the Bear, the gentle breeze of bright Zeus.

Were there no sun, other stars would still kindle kind night.

The sun is new each day.

Some consider Thales the first to study the logic of the stars, predict the time of the eclipse, and sky's turning—so says Eudemos in his history of astrologers. For this very reason, Xenophanes and Herodotus express their wonder; Heraclitus and Democritus likewise bear witness to the same.

Necessity weaves itself truly through the heavens entire, and the solar eclipse, and the combinations both martial and musical— so time is not simply motion but, as I said, holds a motion like soldiers arranged in rank who march in a circle. Of this the sun is commander and the guard on watch, rules and judges the borders, opens wide and sparks the blaze of altering light, and the seasons, as all things do, bear themselves away; according to Heraclitus, it is no paltry thing, nor small, but is great and overmastering, that the sun works together with the first and ruling god.

The teacher of most people is Hesiod. This man they think knew most things, who didn't even understand what day is or night. Day and night are one.

The god of day and night's kind knowing, of winter and summer, of war and peace, of satiety and hunger, alters as fire alters when spices are thrown in the flames, and is called by the name of each perfume.

If all that is would turn to smoke, noses would do the thinking.

In hell souls smell.

What's cool warms, what's warm cools; what's moist parches, what's dry gets moist.

Disperses and gathers together, approaches and departs.

You cannot step into the same river twice; other waters flow in and upon you.

And Heraclitus chastises the poets for saying that "strife should die out among gods and men." Then there would be no harmony of the deftly spear-sharp and the dull, heavy weight, no life without the suckling breast and the phallus; being is the opposite of being.

War fathers all and of all war is king—makes known both gods and men, makes some slaves and sets others free.

They cannot see how what draws itself apart pulls itself together: bending back is the harmony of bow and of lyre.

And of these very things they search through higher realms for natural causes: Euripides says, "Dry earth lóves rain; and holy heaven, swollen with rain, loves to fall on earth." And Heraclitus says that opposites gather together, that what draws apart becomes beautiful harmony, and that strife births all.

Harmony unheard is stronger than harmony heard.

The greatest things can't be tossed together carelessly.

It is necessary and good for men who write down all they think they know to love wisdom.

It is one and the same, the straight way and the crooked, for those who card the flock's wool.

Asses prefer shit mixed with straw to gold.

Seawater is most pure and stained with blood also most vile—
for fish the sea is sweet and sweet refuge, for men it is bitter,
bitter death.

In shit rejoice.

All beasts by blows are driven to pasture.

As of the lyre and the bow, the cosmos is a harmony drawn back.

The good and bad are one. Those doctors, says Heraclitus, cut,
cauterize, question as they cruelly torture the sick, begging
from them a fee undeserved, working for their own gain taken
from such anguish.

What joins together is whole and not whole, intermingling and
pulling apart, marriage that is a divorce: out of all things one
and from one all things.

If not for these things, the name of Justice had not been known.

Indecent, they say, that the gods delight in war. But it's not indecent: finding delight in noble deeds. Wars and battles that seem to us so terrible, these things are not terrible for the gods. For the harmony of the universe entire the god bring all to proper ends, manage the household's many chores; so Heraclitus says, that for gods everything is beautiful and good and just, but men have supposed some things unjust and some just.

It is necessary to know that war is common to all and that strife is just; and we are born of strife and suffering.

Fate fixes all things.

Death is what wakes us and calls us forth, and sleep is what puts us to rest.

The only and only wisdom wants and doesn't want to be spoken in the name of Zeus.

The bow has the name of life and is the work of death.

The deathless are the dying, the dying are the deathless—one lives the other's death, one dies the other's life.

Growing moist is death for the soul, as soil in water dissolves into death—but out of earth water comes, and out of water comes the soul.

The road up and the road down are one road.

The beginning and the end are in common.

The soul's end you cannot find though you walked every path searching, it is so deep a *logos*.

Souls delight in getting wet.

When a man is drunk, a boy with soft cheeks can lead him away and trip him up; he doesn't understand how he takes a step, his soul so full of moisture.

A dry soul is wisest and best.

A dry heat soul is wisest and best.

Where the earth is dry heat, the soul is wisest and best.

Man is kindled, as at night a light, and snuffed out.

When is death not in us? As Heraclitus says, "Life and death, these are one; so are wakefulness and sleep; so are youth and old age; the last falls down into the first, and the first transforms into the latter."

Time is a child playing checkers.

I sought myself.

Into the same river we step and we do not step; we are and we are not.

It is hard work's pain to toil for the same people who rule over you.

In altering it rests.

When the wine isn't stirred the posset's oats and grated cheese separate.

Cast out your ghosts before you dump the shit from your chamber pot.

Those born wish to live and to have their fates—mostly they want to go to sleep and leave behind them children born to their own dooms.

Men reading "youth" think that thirty years makes a generation. As Heraclitus says, that is time enough to give birth to himself as a father, by bearing a child of his own.

The number thirty belongs most deeply to nature's hidden ways—the three and ten are hidden alone in thirty. And the cycle of the moon is constrained and follows only these four numbers in successive order, 1, 4, 9, 16. So hold nothing against Heraclitus the Obscure when he calls the moon a generation.

We all work together toward one total end, some knowingly and with understanding, others knowing nothing at all—I think, says Heraclitus, even the sleepers are workers laboring together to bring forth the world.

It is common to all, to try to make sense of things. Men need to speak their minds to grasp what belongs to everyone, as a city must cling strongly to its many laws. All human laws nurse and grow on that one law of the gods—it rules as far as it wishes to rule, suffices for all, and never is depleted.

One needs to follow after what is common. The *logos* is what is shared, but most men live as if they hold on to an understanding that is only their own.

Most of us endlessly battle the burden we spend our whole lives bearing.

We must not act and speak as if we were asleep.

Heraclitus says, for those who are awake the world is one and common to all; but sleepers each return to a world of their own.

It is human nature not to understand this place of being human; it is for the gods to understand.

Man is called child by the spirits divine, just as a child is by a man.

And does not Heraclitus, as you urge him to, say that the wisest man is but an ape compared to a god's wisdom, beauty, and every other thing?

You don't understand what Heraclitus knows well; that the noblest of apes is a wretch when brought beside animals of other kinds, and the most beautiful pots with swelling bellies are shameful when compared to an innocent girl, just as Hippias says, that wise man.

The people must fight for the law as they'd war with weapons.

Greater fates win greater dooms.

Those slain in war both gods and men honor.

More than a burning fire, you must put out your pride.

Men don't become better by getting what they want. Disease makes health a delight; evil, good; hunger, surfeit; toil, rest.

It's hard to fight against the heart's desires—to get what it wants it bargains away the soul.

All men should seek to know themselves and to chasten their minds.

To have an honest handle on your mind is the highest virtue, and wisdom is to speak the truth and to do as nature allows.

To hide your ignorance is best—hard work when relaxing over wine.

Better to hide your ignorance than to bring it out bare in the middle of things.

Law obeys one's advice.

What mind or heart is theirs? The people follow singers and for teachers want the crowd, not understanding that most men are bad, and just a few are good. The best grasp one thing among everything, a fame everlasting among those who must die, but most men, like sheep, stuff their mouths full.

In Priene lived Bias, son of Teutamas, whose *logos* is more complete than others.

One man for me is more than countless thousands, if he is a true man.

The Ephesians deserve to strangle themselves, those men in their prime, and leave the city to boys, for they cast out Hermodoros, the most useful man among them, saying: "We'll have none among us who are better than ourselves, and if there is such a man, let him be elsewhere among others."

Dogs bark at whom they do not know.

What bears no belief cannot be known.

A fool flutters at every word.

The trusted one knows to keep watch on what seems relevant— and yet justice apprehends the makers of lies and false witnesses.

He said that Homer deserved to be cast out of the poetry contests and beaten with a stick, and Archilochus the same.

It is a law, god-given, that a man lives inside himself. Character
is fate.

For those whose lives have come to an end something patient
waits, unthinkable, and beyond our hopes.

One must wake up and rise and become a guard of the living
and the dead.

Night-wanderers, enchanters, god-frenzied revelers, wild drunks
at the holy tun, you are the initiated.

The laws men make about the mysteries are unholy to the initiates.

And to these statues they utter prayers out loud, as if gossiping in any house, not one knowing anything of what gods and
heroes truly are.

If it weren't for Dionysus that they stepped forward in songs of praise and hymns, the performance would be most shameful. But Hades and Dionysus are the same, for whom the worshippers frenzy and celebrate the holy drunken rites.

Of sacrifices I posit two kinds. First, the pure all-everything cleansing, rare for anyone, as Haraclitus says, that happened to few of us. Second, those involving matter and flesh, formed through change, such as are proper for those bound and held together by the body.

Repairs. Cures. Mendings.

Defiled, they purify themselves with blood, as if one who stepped in mud could wash himself clean with more mud.

Xenophanes

From the age of twenty-five, and for the next sixty-seven years, Xenophanes wandered through Greece, reading his poems to those who would listen. The poems that survive, all in fragments, reveal a poet of a sharp philosophic mind—and by sharp, I mean not only the acute insight the poetry offers but also the honed edge of satire that cuts through it. He mocks Homer and Hesiod for teaching us that the gods behave as we do: shamefully. He chides Pythagoras for that philosopher's claim of continuous memory through many different lives, recognizing in the bark of a dog the voice of an old friend from lifetimes ago.

But in that mockery lurks a subtle revolution in thought. He notes a tendency in humankind to paint the absolute other as a portrait of ourselves—those gods, so like us in their unthinkable unlikeness. We offer potencies we cannot fathom the limits we find within ourselves. Xenophanes will have none of it. Iconoclast to popular opinion in ways that Socrates will fully embody (and fully suffer the consequences of), Xenophanes begins to posit a god or a God of another kind: kin to no human, kin to no creature at all. As Diogenes Laertius puts it: a sphere that "is the totality of mind and thought and is eternal." It is a new thread in the weave of Greek thought, one that Anaxagoras and Empedocles work into the tapestry of their own concerns, considering the world as originating from something other than the elements, from Mind, from Love, from Strife. Xenophanes claims there are many worlds, but none exist at the same time; he says soul is a form of breath; he reminds us that what breathes is also what dies.

Some say he had no teachers; others say this is not true. Boton of Athens taught him, or Archelaus. Born in Colophon, but banished, he lived in Sicily, Elea, and Catania. Then he roamed. It is said he was sold into slavery but freed by two followers of Pythagoras. He felt few things in life become thinkable. And some things in life become unbearable: he buried his sons with his own hands.

He lived a long life. And though most accounts consider the tale spurious, it offers such a gentle ending to a hard life that it bears repeating, a kind of epitaph: At the age of ninety-two he founded a school of philosophy in Elea and lived out the remainder of his days in Hieron's court.

FRAGMENTS

I will imagine these things as being like the truth . . .

⸗

What is clear is this: no one has seen what is—
the fact of the gods and all things of which I speak.
The man who speaks with greatest certainty
　　of what chance has brought into being—
he doesn't know who he is. Of all things, belief builds itself.

The gods are given birth to, so humans think—
and wear clothing, speak, and have bodies like their own.

The gods of the Ethiopians are flat nosed and black;
the Thracians say their gods exist: blue-eyed, red-haired.

If horses and oxen and lions had hands
and with their hands could draw and do all that we do,
horses as horses, and oxen as oxen,
would draw the forms of the gods, each god's
body bearing the shape of the one who drew it.

Homer and Hesiod tattle about all the gods do,
things which, among humans, are blemish and blame—
thievery, adultery, deceit.

The gods didn't, at the beginning, offer mortals all things—
but in time, question by question, we discover more, more truly.

God is one, among gods and humans greatest,
not like mortals in body, not like mortals in thought.

All of him sees, every sense thinks, all of him listens.

On eternal pause he waits, never moving,
not going among others, never seen here, then there.

It takes no effort—with mind and heart he strikes
the all-bell cosmos, and it rings.

$$\diamond$$

From ur-seed to the flow of flower
all things that are, are earth and water.

The sea is water's flowing source, flowing source of wind—
nor can the strong winds blowing out the clouds
come to be without the open ocean's great expanse,
nor the streaming rivers, nor the rain dropping water from the sky.
But the great ocean is mother of clouds of winds
and also of rivers.

The upper crust of the earth can be seen and touches the air;
below the earth is limitless, an infinite reach.

$$\diamond$$

If god had not made golden honey
the fig would be sweetest.

She whom they call Iris, this is just a cloud grown large,
purple and dark red and pale green to see.

And when Pythagoras passed men thrashing a puppy
    he felt pity, they say, and said these words:
"Stop! Don't strike him with that stick! He has the soul
    of an old friend. I recognize him, hearing his voice."

From earth all things come, in earth all things end.

Parmenides, Anaxagoras, Empedocles

Time's endless irony leaves us shockingly little of the life
of Parmenides given the large influence his thinking bears
forward across millennia. Student of Xenophanes but no
follower of his teacher's doctrine, Parmenides wrote a single
poem in epic meter on the nature of what *is* as revealed to him
by the goddess Truth. The name of the goddess in Greek is revelation itself—Ἀλήθεια. The privative α negates λήθε, making of
truth a not-forgetting, a non-oblivion. This disclosedness is the
truth of what is true. It is what reveals itself as it is—a riddle
all the more riddling for the hint that in truth itself what is
revealed will be concealed again, or that some obscurity lurks
inside being's shining brightness. There is a path to follow
to find truth, but there are many paths that look true yet are
not. The senses can give us the miracle-fact of the world,
but the senses also deceive. Soul and mind are one. As are
the evening star and the morning star: they are one, a truth
Parmenides discovered. So say some.

We know he came to Athens to speak. He was an old man
when he spoke, and Socrates sat listening, a young one.

Considered the parent of metaphysics, Parmenides's philosophy informs many of the twentieth century's most prominent
philosophers, Hegel, Heidegger, Russell, and Quine among them.
Fanciful though it may be, Shakespeare's Hamlet is student of
Parmenides when he utters his most famous line, "To be, or not to
be, that is the question"—a question which is no question at all.

Among the lives of all the philosophers I've read, Parmenides's
alone has no death-lore. Perhaps it is because his thinking proves
the most living thought among the truly ancient.

We find him instead on a path of infinite repeat, an image he gives us himself: horses pulling him down truth's singing road, young girls for his guides. If what *is* is an infinite path, those hooves even now gallop down song's fundamental dirt. They are there, those steeds, in the rhythm of the poem, as is the truth they are running toward.

§

Mind governs a cosmos of an infinite number of things infinitely small and infinitely large—so says the man whose nickname in the ancient world was Mind. Student of Anaximenes, whose philosophy of *boundlessness* birthed infinite notions in his pupil, Anaxagoras becomes one of the first philosophers to posit some form or force of *nous* as patterning principle of the universe entire, whose nature makes of the infinite all a *One*.

He forsook the wealth of his patrimony and, asked if he had no love for his fatherland, he said he did and pointed up at the blue sky.

Sky clear, he sat down and wrapped a cloak around him; then the rain arrived.

Given time, he said, the mountains will turn to sea.

Meteors are stones falling from the sun. The sun itself, he says, is not a god but a molten clod large as the Peloponnese.

It is that last assertion about the nature of the sun that makes of Anaxagoras a proto-Socrates. He is brought to trial for impiety. The single braid of his life story separates into different strands. In one version, his student Pericles defends him, and the philosopher is fined five talents and sent into exile. In a version of the same, Pericles defends him, and the philosopher is released, but is so angered at his mistreatment that he kills himself. In the last, he is accused not only of impiety but treasonable communication with the Persians. (When he was a young man, Xerxes attacked.) Judged guilty, Anaxagoras and his sons were sentenced to death. His response: nature long ago condemned both him and his judges to death; and that he knew that his sons were born only to die.

The stones that are stars will fall down if the cosmos stops spinning. So says Mind in the circuits of his thinking.

The road to death, Mind says, is the same from wherever you start.

Mind died at the age of seventy-two.

٭

A gloomy man in glorious robes, luxuriant hair circled by a laurel crown, Empedocles walked melancholy through the world wearing bronze sandals and a golden sash, followed by a retinue of acolytes. He came by his flamboyance naturally. Born into a wealthy family on Agrigentum in Greek Sicily, his famous grandfather—a victor in the seventy-first Olympiad—raised horses. But with his money he did wonderful things that tell also of the nature of the man: to poor brides he gave a dowry.

That largesse is kind, but its kindness exceeds the social sphere of wedding and marriage. At the core of Empedocles's philosophy are two fundamental gods, more *forces* or *potencies* or *laws* than gods typically understood: Love and Strife. These primal opposites cycle through the cosmos entire. When Love dominates, being gathers and generates; when Strife dominates, life's intimate braid is undone. Love's reign unfolds into peace unfathomable; Strife curses the mouth with the blood of its sustenance. A little money spent to further love in the daily world might well further Love in the cosmos. So you pay for the dowry.

This idea of Empedocles, of Love and Strife, bears within it the realizations of thinkers before him who also questioned, if not ridiculed, the typical notions of the gods—those beings so often behaving in ways we'd be ashamed to behave ourselves. There is echo here of Parmenides's goddess Truth, whose thinkable path is the only path there is. But one also hears Pythagoras and his eternal numbers; Xenophanes, whose hexameters sing out the One; Anaxagoras's world governed by Mind. The ancient commentaries claim Empedocles studied with each thinker, though the realities of time pull the rumors apart. It is said he studied with Pythagoras but was caught plagiarizing and exiled from further discussions; others say he took the living dialogue and wrote it down in verse, and for this outrage—which says as much about the nature of poetry as it does person—was forced to leave the philosophic sect. But other commentators claim he studied with Xenophanes or, together with Zeno, with Parmenides. What feels true to say is this: he bears in his thinking the intricate lacework of the thinkers before him, and he wanders out into the world, singing his thoughts.

But he is more than a thinker. The raiment of wondrous tale adorns the man as closely as does his other finery. It is said he could perform magic. Once, when the winds blew so hard in their force they flayed the crops, Empedocles gave this advice: sacrifice their asses and from their skins make bags. Then he took the bags, stretched them open on the surrounding hills, caught the winds, and saved the harvest. A woman dead thirty days he brought back to life. At a dinner a young man angered by the host grabbed his sword; Empedocles grabbed his lyre, sang a song to soothe the passion of the young man, saved the life of the host, and saved the young man from committing murder. That young man became Empedocles's most renowned disciple.

He lived for sixty years, says Aristotle; but others say he lived well past one hundred. Nor is there any single story about his death. He fell and broke his thigh, and, in the illness that followed, died. It seems plausible enough: a mortal story for a mortal man. But Empedocles thought he had himself become a god. After the feast of a sacrifice conducted in a field, his friends went off to rest. A loud voice called out Empedocles's name, and when his friends awoke and sought him, the sky was lit up as if by torches, but the philosopher was gone. But it is also said that he left the sacrifice and walked to Mount Etna, the volcano beneath which the monster Typhon lies furious and chained, and in order to prove the rumor true, that he was indeed a god, walked to the crater's edge and jumped in. He has no grave. No remains. Just one bronze sandal hurled back out of the flames.

PARMENIDES

—for Sally Keith

> ... the common for me is
> Where one should begin: there the ancient arrives as new.

First of all gods she devised the fundamental Eros

Come, and I'll speak. The myth you'll hear will be your own—
The only paths of inquiry are those you see to think:
What is *is*, and of what *is*, it cannot not be—
This is Persuasion's path (and Truth follows after).
And of what *is not*, it must be what cannot be,
I'm pointing out to you the path inscrutable—
No knowing the unperceivable *is not* (no, not possible),
And no, you can't speak it.

Horses carried me off. As far as my blood-beating mind wanted,
They brought me. They took me down that road of many songs,
The goddess's road, that brings the knowing man shining to
    all towns.
So I came here: horses with heads full-of-thoughts strained full
    speed
To bring me—budding girls leading the way.
From the axle in the axle box a note as if played by a flute
Blazed out, and two wheels, whirling circles, pressed hard
On either side. The daughters of the Sun were in a hurry
To escort me, leaving behind their house of Night
For the light, their hands casting the veils from their faces.
There is the gate of the roads of Night and Day,
This gate has a lintel above, and below, a threshold made of
    stone.
The heavens themselves are full of large doors,
And much-punishing Justice holds the keys that fit those locks.
The girls, with soft words, charmed her—
Carefully persuading her to throw the bar
Quickly from the gates. The doors opening
Created a vast chasm, countless bronze pins
In hinges one by one in turn rolling back,
Fit to posts with bolts and rivets. Then and there, straight
    ahead
The girls took the chariot and horses down the high road.
And the goddess received me kindly, took my right hand
In her hands, and spoke these words meant for me:
"Young man, who is as if wedded to these deathless drivers
Whose horses brought you here to my home,
Welcome. It was no evil fate that sent you to come
Down this road, so far from the paths most men walk,
But Law and Justice brought you. I want you to learn all—

Both Truth's pulsing, never-trembling heart
And what mortals suppose true, in which there is no truth, no
    faith.
But somehow this thing you'll learn—that all that seems to be
Most truly is, all everything that seems to be, it's true: is,
    is.
What is needed to speak, to perceive, is what *is.* What is *is* to
    be,
What nothing *is* is not, the not-is—I'm urging you: ponder it.
But first, I hold you back from the path you're seeking—
Bar you from that road down which mortals knowing nothing
Make their way, two-headed. You are lost in yourself—
Breast's tangle of desire, mind astray. Others make their way,
Deaf and blind, labyrinthine, a mob minus a mind,
For whom coming to be and being nothing are considered
The same, all of them are turned aside from this path.

One path's myth yet
Remains, that which *is*. On this path are many omens,
Many signs, that uncreated cannot be destroyed;
Is is whole, is singular, untrembling and without end.
Never a *when* when it was or will be, when *now* is all, the same
Continuous one, coherent, flowing.
                              What ask it of its own origin?
How ask from where it grew? Not from what is not, I won't
Let you say that, nor think it—it is unspeakable, unthinkable,
That what *is* somehow is not. What need called it forth—
Not late, not early, beginning from nothing—to grow?
Fate's need: that it must fully be, or not at all.
Faith's brute force won't first bring being to be—
What births itself? Justice reaches a point: what *is*
Can neither come to be nor perish. She loosens her shackles,
But holds fast. The crisis of all these things is this:
Is or *is-not*. But the choice has been made, as is necessary—
Not to go down the unthinkable, nameless way (this is not
Truth's path), but this way, where being comes to be and is
    real.
How could what *is* remain undone? How could it come to be?
For if it came to be, then once it wasn't, it was never
    destined to be.
So genesis is a bright idea put out, and ruin never heard of.
It's not divided up in parts, since all is the same;
No one thing most worthy: that would stop its gathering
    together;
No one thing is the worst: all is full of being.
A continuity, all of it *is*; being draws near to being.
But is immovable, bound within strongest limits,
Is without beginning, never-ending, since genesis and ruin
Far away have been banished, repulsed by Truth's good faith.

The same is stable in the same, by itself it rests
And so rooted there, remains; and that fierce god Necessity
Binds it within strict limits, and all around it is shut in.
It is sanctified and just, that what is is not incomplete—
That it lacks nothing, for if it lacked anything, it would lack
     all.
(To perceive this thing also thinks this thought, *it is*—
For it's not without being, what we have been told of,
And in it you'll find knowing, for nothing is or is to be
Other than what presents itself as being, because Fate's
     fetters
Binds it motionless and whole. *Is* is the name
All mortals have learned and been persuaded is true—
All that bursts into life and falls apart, all that is and then isn't,
That changes shape, bright colors altering into bright light.)
But since there is a furthest edge, on every side
It is complete, a massive sphere like a child's bubble,
Every edge equidistant from the center—it must be
No part here grows larger, no part there smaller.
There isn't what is-not—for it would stop reaching
Into its likeness—nor is what *is* somehow more here
And less there, not stronger or weaker, for all is inviolate:
Equal on all sides to itself, exactly full to its utmost edge.

Now I stop my honest words and glimpsing thoughts
About Truth—now you'll learn the dying ideas of mortal men
Listening to my words altered into a cosmic delusion.
They set their duplicitous minds to name two forms
When naming one is wrong—these men led into getting lost—
Dividing opposites into living bodies and grave signs.
One split from the other: the bright aether-air's pure fire,
Gentle, weightless, light loosely woven, equal to itself

Everywhere, but equal to no other. But there is that other
Opposing one: an unknowing night, a dense body clumsily
    built.
The universal order as it naturally appears I describe to you,
So that mere mortal thoughts never unnerve you.

No, never be seduced by this thought: that what is-not, is—
But you, I shut your sight from this path's questioning,
And never let habit's too-much experience march you down it,
Guiding you with unfocused eyes aimless and ears and tongue
Ringing loud, but judge with logic this much-scrutinized test,
Spoken out by me.

As each person is a tangle of limbs always moving
So the mind is placed in humans. The thing itself
That thinks shares the same nature of those limbs
For each and every person—

You will know aether's nature and all the aethereal
Signs, the dark work the pure, alert, bright, torch sun does.
These annihilating deeds from which life emerges
You'll learn, and you'll learn the nature of the round moon's
Wandering ways; you will know all the surrounding heavens
Hold, what sprung into being, and how Necessity
Shackled the stars to their limits.

            . . . how earth and sun and moon,
The common air, the Milky Way's milk, and Olympus
So high, so far, and the soul-like might of stars rushed
Into being . . .

The narrow straits filled with the absolute flame,
Others around those full of night, some fire set within them,
And in the middle of these, the divine one who drives all—
She rules over the hated birth and intercourse of all things,
Sending the male to mix with the female and also the opposite,
The female with the male.

But since all things are named daylight and dark night
And by their own potency belong to one or the other,
All is full of both bright day and night's hidden obscure,
Both equal, both together, neither more, neither less.

In this way, as we all know, these things that grew now are,
And nourished to full life, will afterward come to their end—
And humans have stamped down, as on a coin, names on
    each one.

Sharp eye forever searching for the sun's day-bright beam . . .

Gaze in on all that is absent but still rooted in the mind—
You won't be cut away from being if you hold on to what is—
Not scattered blindly everywhere through the cosmos—
Not thrown together.

What is is what is

for thinking and also

for being

The night-sheen around the earth a strange light leaping . . .

ANAXAGORAS

—*for Sasha Steensen*

What you see is a vision of what cannot be seen.

How can hair sprout from what is not hair, and how can flesh form from what is not skin?

Because of our weakness we are not able to discern the truth.

In everything is a portion of all things, except in the Mind. (But some things are in the Mind, too.)

Everything was one, all matter in common, limitless and count-less and small—for the small things too are infinite. And when all was in common, nothing could be seen, the smallness of being being so small. Air and aether hold power over all, both being without limit. Within the whole these two are largest, in plenitude and magnitude both.

Of the small there is no smallest, but smaller yet always exists (for what *is* is not *not* to be). And of the great there is always a greater, equal in number to the small. But each to itself is both great and small.

And the air and aether grow separate from the surrounding throng, and that manyness has no limit.

Nothing falls apart from any other thing in the cosmic whole, nothing can be hewn off with a battle-ax, not the hot from the cold, not the cold from the hot.

And then Mind sets all things in motion; this motion causes everything to separate, dividing one from another, and this rotation creates more and more division.

All other things share some inner portion, but the Mind is boundless and self-ruling and joined to no other substance, but only it is alone—alone in itself. If not wholly in and of itself, what of mind would mix with what, everything sharing a portion of all other things, but it is as I've said before. For if matter weren't hindered from mingling with Mind, it could rule nothing in the way it does—alone and within itself.

Finer than a husked millet seed and of all substances most pure, it thinks every thought about all things and is most powerful. And whatever has some portion of soul, the Mind rules it all—the larger and the lesser.

And the all-at-once rotation of the whole the Mind rules, so that from the beginning it rotated. First it began to rotate in a small way, but then the rotation grew larger, and will grow larger yet.

And the mingling together and the pulling apart and the gathering separations (as of the three plaits parted to braid hair) all are known by Mind. And Mind made the musical order of all things—of what was and what is not, of what is and what will be—and set spinning those now circling around, the stars and sun and moon, and Mind divided the air from aether. This rotation itself created the separating force.

And Mind divides slender from thick and cold from hot and misty gloom from piercing light and the vital from the withered.

There are many portions of many things. Nothing is wholly separate, nothing is divided off one from another, except for

Mind. Mind is one—the larger and the smaller. But nothing else is like any other thing, but each is obviously that thing of which it contains the most.

And since the portions (as if fated) of the large and the small are equal in amount, all things would be in everything—nothing set apart is ever to be, but a portion of everything is mixed in all. And since no power is able to separate, what is smallest cannot be, but from the beginning of time to now, all is the same. In all things are many things, and of what can be divided, the larger and the smaller, there is an equal amount.

These things having been separated in this way, it's necessary to know that all things are not less or more (for how can there be more than all), but all things are always equal.

For these things rotate and come apart by force and speed—force that speed creates—and their swiftness is like nothing now found among humans, but all is exponentially quicker.

These things being so, one must imagine that there are many things of all kinds, everything being interwoven, and seeds and substances and forms of every kind, every flavor, and all delights.

And humans also were joined together, as were the other creatures who possessed a soul; and friendship bound people together in clans, and together they worked the fields, just as with us; and for them the sun and the moon burned bright, just as for us; and for them the earth sprouted each and every green thing; and they gathered those they wanted, brought them home, and used them. These things I'm speaking of, this separating off one from another, didn't happen to us alone, but also to others.

Before that time when each thing became exactly itself, all being was the same, no color visible, difference was naught, for matter all intermingled prevented it—the wet and the dry (river's flow and arroyo, bird's liquid song and the empty air), the hot and the cold, the starbright and the nether-gloom, much earth in the substance and an endless number of seeds, not one like another. And nothing among the other things either, not one is like to the other.

These things being this way, it's necessary to suppose that all substance holds within it the whole.

The dense and wet and cold and dark came together and now are here, in the earth, and the rarefied and hot and dry drift out into the aether.

From the separation of these things, earth is put together; water is shed from clouds, and earth comes of water; cold compresses earth to stones, and the stones move farther away than water does.

The Greeks always think crookedly about life and death—for nothing comes to be and nothing dies away, but being's very substance gathers together and falls apart. This is clear thinking: to call life this gathering together, to call death this falling apart.

. . . because of our weakness we are not able to discern the truth . . .

. . . what you see is a vision of what cannot be seen . . .

We call the rainbow that sun-defying brightness in the clouds.

The sun put its lamp in the moon.

EMPEDOCLES

—for Kylan Rice

First, listen. These are the four roots of all things—
lightning-bright Zeus and life-bearing Hera; blind Hades;
and Hunger, whose tears weep mortal streams.

Friends, I know there is truth in the tales
I sing out loud—but it brings trouble, I know,
for women and men, whose minds distrust
    being told to trust.

When the divine was mixed with greater divinity,
and one thing met another, they crashed together,
the birth of many things an unbroken perpetuity.

I'll tell you another thing: in nature there is never
all dying, the world doesn't end in one final wretched death—
but only mixing, separating, and gathering up again
is what is. What humans name nature is this motion.

I'll say it again: every mortal thing is birthed.
Nor do all things end in cursed death—
but mixture and separation of things mixed
is all that is "nature," a mortal name humans gave.

Never in the whole-holy-All is anywhere empty—
    and never can more come to be than is.

From nothing, nothing comes—
to die utterly away is impossible, unheard of—
wherever you push on eternity, eternity is always there.

Earth gives of earth, air of air.

In the no-world below many fires burn.

Aether's long roots plunge beneath the earth.

Only those with roots densely tangled send up
their spray of scattered shoots, birthing blooms above.

... and so the tall trees lay their eggs, the wild olives first.

... and fig juice curdles and binds white milk.

... and what is lawful for all is a thread pulled tight
through the wide aether, the boundless sun's bright rays.

... saffron's bright streak on linen.

... never to say there is in life only one path.

ϛ

But gods, turn away the madness from my tongue,
and from pious lips pull a pure spring of living water.
And you, white-armed virgin, Muse much-wooed,
meet me kindly: and what law allows one with so short a life
    to hear,
send Piety with those words, as you drive, tame to reins,
    the chariot.
And for you, whoever you are, may the Muse never force
    you to pluck those flowers
mortals honor most, who think it takes courage to say
more than is permitted to say, hurrying to wisdom's heights.
But come, look as you can look at each clear thing,
never trusting sight more than you trust listening,
nor any echoing sound, over the tongue's plainsong;
never trust those others, though in some way they seem
    to open a path for thought—
hold back your arms, your legs. Think about the clarity
    of each given thing.

On earth we see earth, water in water,
aether in heavenly aether, ruinous fire in fire,
motherly love in Love, mournful strife in Strife.

I speak in doubles: at that time the one and only grew holy
into many; then what was many grew into what is one.
Twofold the way mortals come to be; twofold how they die.
The gathering into one births a world it also destroys;

the other motion works backward, a germinated seed
    that splits apart as it grows.
And these transformations, all through each, never cease—
now Love gathers all things into one,
then each is torn apart again by Strife's hatred.
This they've learned: many grow into one
and what is one breaks back into many. Coming to an end
and coming to be, their life is no eon-root gripped firm
    in the ground,
but these changes, all through each, never stop,
are endless, eternal, a cycle that cannot be broken.
Come, listen to the words that leap from my lips,
    learning strengthens the mind's heart, heart's mind.
As I said before, marking the limits of my words,
I speak in doubles: at that time what was many grew
into a holy one; then what was one grew into many—
fire and water and earth and air's boundless height,
cursed Strife split apart from them, and is found equally
    everywhere,
but Love also among them, equal in length and breadth.
Look with your mind; never let amazement sit in your eyes.
For mortals she is believed to be born in the joints
    of human limbs,
and through her they think lovingly and do friendly deeds,
her nickname is Joy, and they call her Aphrodite.
No mortal man has seen her dancing among them—
so I've taught. Listen to my words on their journey;
    they don't deceive.
Fire, water, earth, air—these all are equal everywhere
    and were born at the same time.
Each rules, honored by the others, its singular abode;

each rules, for a time, Time's revolutions.
And of these elements, nothing more after them is born,
    nor do they cease—
for falling forever into ruin, what could come to be?
What could diminish this singular all? Where would it go?
How perish, when there is no reft realm, no desolate void?
But these elements are what is, all woven through each,
at one time becoming one thing, at another time, another—
    yet bearing out forever always the same.

[*a description of the god*]

Two branches don't thrust up out his back,
he has no feet, he does not suddenly weep,
    and no, not at all, he is not born—
but equal on all sides, wholly without limit,
a globe made round by spinning round,
    in love with his own solitude.

But Strife grew large in limb,
and when time bloomed open he sprang to honor—
a broad oath exchanged and put in motion.
One after another all
    things struck by Strife's
        hand tremble.

But I will return and set out on that path of song—
those first told, words drawn off from other words
far away: When Strife reached the vortex's deepest
depth, Love came to be in the middle of the whirl,
and here, all things join, and become a singular *is*,
not at once, but by will slowly interwoven, each through
    the other.
And as all these joined together, myriad mortal things
    (such tears) flowed out,
and those unmixed stood out contrary to those mixing
    together,
and all this Strife subdued, held up aloft, apart—not yet
    had he
ended his guiltless retreat to the sphere's utmost edge,
but he remained in some limbs still, not yet fully withdrawn.
As far as he ran always ahead, just so far followed always
gentle-minded Love—blameless, immortal—rushing after.
So suddenly the deathless things learned how to die,
isolate-pure before being mixed, now one path exchanged
    for another.
Mixed together, the myriad mortal things (so like tears)
    flowed out,
each and every one fitted to its form—to witness is wonder.
Earth was there, and Sun farseeing,
bloodstained Battle, and sober-eyed Harmony,
Beauty and Shame, Swiftness and Long-Time,
Certainty and dark-haired Doubt,
    and also the Great Obscure.

Growth and Withering, Sleep and Wakefulness,
Motion and Stillness, Greatness wearing many garlands,
and Filth, Wisdom, and Prophecy.

Formed inside the broad-chested earth
of the eight portions, two obtained from Nestis,
    in the death-queen's dream-light sheen,
and four from Hephaestus—white bones were born,
sewn sweetly together by divine Harmony.

. . . and the hungry lions who sleep on the ground in the hills
came to be, the sweet bay and the olive tree with lovely tresses . . .

. . . and at last, seers and singers, healers
and leaders, come to be among the earthly—
and then, like the flowers' green fuse, the blossom,
    the gods, greatest and most honored . . .

Strife accursed

                    and tenacious Love

Now listen: how men and women, much-lamented,
buds in the gloom, were led to sprout by fire as it grew
    apart—
learn these glories—my words aren't ignorant, they
    do not look away.
Clods molded by the earth first sprung out as forms,
having a portion of both moisture and heat—
fire urged them up to seek out their like,
lovely limbs not yet unfurled to frame their bodies,
no birth cry, no battle cry, no voice at all—
    no words native to humankind.

They are one, all things in themselves in every part,
blazing sun and earth, sky and the saltwater sea,
but among mortals, this gift: they strayed, and grew apart.

By Love's love, many heads—on no stems, no necks—
    sprouted up into buds,
naked arms groped near, not bedded in shoulders,
and eyes wandered blind, without faces.

. . . a boy, a girl—once I'd been born a boy and a girl—
and a bush and a hawk and also leaping out the sea
    a silent, scaly fish . . .

Narrow is the cunning life coursing through our limbs—
many the miseries that strike dull our thoughtful cares,
having seen by living only the swift flight away of life—
each leaves, early to death, drifting off like smoke,
persuaded wholly by each thing they encounter,
driven at once in every direction. But who boasts
    he has found the whole?
For humans, the whole is never seen, never heard—
for the mind it's past understanding. But since,
    from the straight path you've strayed here,
you'll learn: mortal wisdom has flown no further.

The drugs that cure ailments and hold off old age
You'll learn—for you alone I will do all this.
You'll stop the endless, angry winds roused around
the earth, blasting the planted fields, crop wasting away—
and in turn, if you wish, to requite the gale, you'll bring
    a gentle breeze;
you'll dry up the deluge of dark clouds thundering,
and for us will also put a flow through summer's drought
that flowers into fruit trees—in the aether, they'll take root.
You'll bring out from Hades the soul of a dead man.

But what idiots care for never reaches far—
hoping that what never was will come to be,
assuming that what dies is destroyed forever.

No wise man in his mind would dare divine this—
that for as long as they live what they call a life,
for they are just as they are, the wretched and the good,
and before their dust gathers into bodies, and after
they are undone, there is this nothing.

It is proclaimed necessary, by god's ancient decree,
eternal, made fast by broad oaths—
when from fear one fails, he defiles his lovely limbs,
and from that failure follows the holy oath sworn false;
then souls gain a life long-lasting, but not immortal,
three times, for endless hours, they stray from bliss's blessing,
born into time and every mortal form,
life changes into this painful path—
from air tossed down to angry sea,
from sea crushed to earth's edge, from earth to the sun's
dawn-day blinding shine, then thrown into the whirling
    eddies of the air—
each from the others is taken, each grown hateful to all.
And now I am among them, too; god's exile, wandering—
all because I put my faith in Strife's madness.

§

For god they didn't have some Ares or Din-of-Battle,
no Zeus-king, no Cronos, no Poseidon,
but Queen Cypris ...
they appeased her by offering reverent images
of painted animals, sweet perfumes curiously mixed,
burnt myrrh unmixed and pure, frankincense and thyme,
pouring to the ground a sacrifice of golden honey—
slaughter of unblemished bulls never drenched the altars,
but among humans this deed was greatest defilement,
breaking off limb from limb, gorging on life.
All things were tame, gentle to humans,
both beasts and birds of prey, a kindliness
        blazed out brightly.

If only I had died before that pitiless day,
before I devised, by the food I ate,
        miserable deeds with my lips.

A father will lift up, in changed shape, his loved son
and saying a prayer, cut the child's throat—the great fool
        fooled greatly. The others don't understand,
begging on the suppliant's behalf—but the father is deaf
        to their shouts,
slaughters the boy, and in his home, cooks an evil feast.
As the father, so the son. He grabs his mother and children,
breaks apart their lives, and devours their flesh.

... and will not cease from murder's sick sound; don't you see
how, with anguished minds, you devour each other?

And so, angered at their own wicked crimes,
their souls never rest from their wretched wailing.

... weeping and wailing I came to a strange place.

                                  ... a joyless place,
where Murder and Revenge and the other tribes
        of Death-Gods
roam the Meadow of Bewilderment in darkness.

... arrived underneath the roof of this cave ...

... all-covering earth ...

ʂ

Blessed, who gains the gold mine of a mind god-given—
wretched, who cares most for dark doctrines about the gods.

No human head, unarmed by arms,
no feet, no shaggy chest,
     there are for the god none of these,
just a mind, holy and unspeakable, utterly alone,
thoughts rushing across all the cosmos.

For humans—
     the mind grows toward what is present.

As far as they grow different, always in them
arises a different way to think.

As when painters paint votive offerings in many colors,
two men, by art and wise craft they learned so well,
put their hands to the palette's many hues,
harmony made by mixing some more, others less,
and making from them forms resembling all things—
bringing as if into being trees and men and women,
wild beast and omen-birds, and fish living in waters,
even the immortal gods, in honors greatest.

Don't fall prey to this falsehood, that your mind
    comes from some other, unearthly place—
for mortals, the unspeakable is what comes to be,
    pure source,
and know this piercing truth: it is the living word
    of a god you have heard.

As when, mind made up to leave, you prepare a lamp,
bright flame to burn through the winter night,
and seal the glass to guard the lantern against every gust,
glass that shatters the breath of the ever-blowing winds—
and the light leaps out, farthest-reaching,
indestructible beams shining beyond the threshold—
as when long ago, the fundamental fire, sheathed
in fine linen, protected from the deep waters flowing
all around, waits for a young girl's eye to open,
and the fire leaps out to reach in as far as it can reach.

No easy task to obtain what's before our eyes,
our hands' grasp can't grasp it, human minds
fall violently down persuasion's strongest path—
    so does the heart.

If you place the thought-throng in your midmost mind,
and with pure study and long attention think kindly,
they will be with you, these things, for your whole life—

and many others you'll gain. Growing in strength,
these become the place a person is, an ethos dependent
    on each person's nature.
But if you hold out for other sorts of cares
among the myriad miseries of humankind, these thoughts
    grow dim, blunt, dull.
They will darken suddenly away from you as time ambles on,
longing's sweet regret pulling them back to their own kind.
Know this: all things think and have their share of mind.

The heart, nurtured in the blood's echoing ocean,
is where in humans what is best called thought is—
for the blood around the human heart is thought.

Sources

THALES

9   *and according to some* Diogenes Laertius
9   *And among his everlasting* Diogenes Laertius
9   *The first Greeks* Flavius Josephus
10   *And these apothegms* Diogenes Laertius
10   *The divine utterance* Diogenes Laertius
10   *After studying politics* Diogenes Laertius
10   *No one explained* Diogenes Laertius
11   *Pythagoras urged him* Iamblichus
11   *From the Egyptians* Diogenes Laertius
11   *Thales believes* Aëtius
11   *And all things are borne* Hippolytus
11   *You stuck your walking stick* Plutarch
12   *This theory brought* Diogenes Laertius
12   *Hieronomos also says* Diogenes Laertius
12   *Eudemos, in* **The History** Proclus
12   *It is through ancient Thales* Proclus
12   *They say Thales was first* Proclus
12   *He was first to find* Diogenes Laertius
13   *Of the seasons* Diogenes Laertius
13   *Followers of Thales* Aëtius
13   *from earth is* Aëtius
13   *the sun throws* Aëtius
13   *Eudemos records in* **The Astrologies** Theon of Smyrna
13   *Thales first said the sun's eclipse* Aëtius
13   *After he philosophized* Aëtius
14   *The historian Heraclides* Diogenes Laertius
14   *To someone seeking* Diogenes Laertius
14   *When asked why* Diogenes Laertius
14   *"The same gifts"* Diogenes Laertius
14   *Before us or far away* Diogenes Laertius
14   *all things are* Aristotle
15   *When Croesus came* Herodotus
15   *Someone asked what is difficult* Diogenes Laertius
15   *He also seems to have offered* Diogenes Laertius
16   *When the same war raged* Herodotus
16   *Timon knows him also* Diogenes Laertius
16   *Callimachus thought* Diogenes Laertius
16   *of astronomy written* Diogenes Laertius
16   *the stars are earthlike* Aëtius
17   *And Thales, studying* Plato
17   *Scolding him for his poverty* Aristotle
17   *the cosmos is the mind* Aëtius
17   *"Don't get rich,"* Diogenes Laertius
18   *As if the words* Diogenes Laertius

18   *that Thales declared* Aristotle
18   *He said that everything begins* Galen
18   *Thales also says* Aristotle
18   *Nevertheless, not all* Hippolytus
19   *Maybe he grasped this* Aristotle
19   *Some say the soul* Aristotle
19   *Some people say* Diogenes Laertius
19   *Thales first revealed* Aëtius
20   *the cosmos is a corpse* Diogenes Laertius
20   *the world is one* Aëtius
20   *Aristotle and Hippias* Diogenes Laertius
20   *So the wise* Diogenes Laertius
20   *"Death," he said* Diogenes Laertius
20   *His statue bears* Diogenes Laertius

ANAXIMANDER
21   *Anaximander of Miletus* Diogenes Laertius
21   *Anaximander, friend of Thales* Strabo
21   *Anaximander of Miletus, son of Praxiades* Theophrastus
21   *Diodorus of Ephesus* Diogenes Laertius
21   *Eratosthenes says* Strabo
21   *among the Greeks* Themistius
22   *Like a child left* Diogenes Laertius
22   *He wrote* **On Nature** Suda
22   *the unbound heavens* Aëtius
22   *out from the confusion* Aëtius
22   *infinite worlds* Aëtius
22   *the world is full* Aëtius
23   *He was first* Simplicius
23   *And yet it is also* Aristotle
23   *Philosophers who claim* Simplicius
23   *Anaximander says that the source* Aëtius
24   *The other thinkers* Aristotle
24   *Of the philosophers* Aëtius
24   *The philosophers of nature* Aristotle
24   *All those men* Aristotle
24   *It was clear* Simplicius
25   *Anaximander spoke of an element* Simplicius
25   *the fundamental element* Diogenes Laertius
25   *Some thinkers assumed* Aristotle
25   *the sun's circle* Aëtius
25   *it is twenty-eight* Aëtius
26   *when the mouth* Aëtius
26   *the sun is equal* Aëtius
26   *the moon has* Aëtius
26   *the earth is high* Eudemos
26   *In the middle rests* Diogenes Laertius
26   *Some say its likeness* Aristotle

27   *the earth is like* Aëtius
27   *the air, dense* Aëtius
27   *the wind is a flow* Aëtius
27   *Anaximander links* Aëtius
27   *Aristotle included in* Alexander of Aphrodisias
27   *the seas are relict* Aëtius
28   *At first the earthly* Aristotle
28   *These thinkers say* Alexander of Aphrodisias
28   *lightning storm and thunder* Aëtius
29   *After Thales, Anaximander* Pseudo-Plutarch
29   *from the ur-dew* Aëtius
29   *He did not think* Plutarch
30   *Those descended from* Plutarch
30   *This principle* Hippolytus
31   *This man first built* Eusebius
31   *He discovered first* Diogenes Laertius
31   *It is said that the children* Diogenes Laertius

ANAXIMENES
33   *He used to speak* Diogenes Laertius
33   *the sun is* Aëtius
33   *the circling outermost* Aëtius
33   *like nails struck* Aëtius
33   *the moon holds* Theon of Smyrna
33   *fiery indeed is* Aëtius
34   *Anaximenes and Diogenes* Aristotle
34   *Anaximenes, just as* Simplicius
34   *air is revealed* Aëtius
34   *It is necessary* Aëtius
35   *They say Anaximenes* Plutarch
35   *The ancient astrologers* Aristotle
35   *a trapezium* Aëtius
35   *flatness of the earth* Aristotle
36   *The one principle* Pseudo-Olympiodorus
36   *the principal element* Hippolytus
37   *Anaximenes wants to* Pseudo-Galen
37   *He says the drawing* Plutarch
38   *clouds grow fat* Aëtius
38   *the rainbow comes* Aëtius
38   *a rainbow appears* Scholia on Aratus's *Phaenomena*
38   *not one of these* Aëtius
38   *Of meteorological phenomena* Aëtius
39   *Anaximenes says that drenching* Aristotle
39   *The world is made* Simplicius
39 · *dense air* Aëtius
39   *countless worlds* Aëtius
39   *the world* Aëtius
39   *the soul* Aëtius
39   *the air* Aëtius

HERACLITUS

51   *To say as I say isn't wisdom* Hippocrates

XENOPHANES

75   *I will imagine* Plutarch
75   *What is clear* Sextus
75   *The gods are* Clement
75   *The gods of* Clement
76   *If horses and oxen* Clement
76   *Homer and Hesiod* Sextus
76   *The gods didn't* Stobaeus
76   *God is one* Clement
76   *All of him* Sextus
76   *On eternal pause* Simplicius
77   *It takes no effort* Simplicius
77   *From ur-seed* Simplicius
77   *The sea is* Scholiast (Geneva codex)
77   *The upper crust* Achilles
77   *If god had* Herodian
78   *She whom they* Scholiast (Eustatius)
78   *And when Pythagoras* Diogenes Laertius
78   *From earth all* Sextus

PARMENIDES

87   *the common* Proclus
88   *First of all* Simplicius
89   *Come, and I'll* Proclus
90   *Horses carried* Sextus Empiricus
92   *One path's myth* Simplicius
95   *No, never be seduced* Plato
96   *As each person* Theophrastus
97   *You will know* Clement
98   *how earth and sun* Simplicius
99   *The narrower straits* Simplicius
100   *But since all things* Simplicius
101   *In this way* Simplicius
102   *Sharp eye forever* Plutarch
103   *Gaze in on all* Clement
104   *What is is* Clement
105   *The night-sheen* Plutarch

ANAXAGORAS

107   *What you see* Sextus
107   *How can hair* Sextus
107   *Because of our weakness* Scholium on Gregory of Nazianzus
107   *In everything is* Simplicius
107   *Everything was one* Simplicius
108   *Of the small* Simplicius
108   *And the air* Simplicius

108   *Nothing falls apart* Simplicius
108   *And then Mind* Simplicius
109   *All other things* Simplicius
110   *And since the portions* Simplicius
110   *These things having been* Simplicius
110   *For these things* Simplicius
110   *These things being so* Simplicius
111   *The dense and wet* Simplicius
112   *From the separation* Simplicius
112   *The Greeks always* Simplicius
112   **because of our weakness** Simplicius
112   **what you see** Simplicius
112   *We call the rainbow* Scholium on Iliad
112   *The sun put* Plutarch

EMPEDOCLES

113   *First, listen* Aëtius
113   *Friends, I know* Clement of Alexandria
113   *When the divine* Simplicius
113   *I'll tell you* Aëtius
114   *I'll say it again* Aëtius
114   *Never in the whole-holy-All* Philo of Alexandria
114   *From nothing, nothing* Aristotle
114   *Earth gives of earth* Proclus
114   *In the no-world* Aristotle
114   *Aether's long roots* Herodian
115   *Only those with roots* Aristotle
115   *and so the tall* Plutarch
115   *and fig juice* Aristotle
115   *and what is lawful* Plutarch
115   *saffron's bright streak* Plutarch
115   *never to say* Sextus Empiricus
116   *But gods, turn* Aristotle
116   *On earth we see* Simplicius
116   *I speak in doubles* Hippolytus
118   *Two branches don't* Aristotle
118   *But Strife grew* Simplicius
118   *One after another* Simplicius
119   *But I will return* Plutarch
120   *Growth and Withering* Cornutus
120   *Formed inside* Simplicius
120   *and the hungry lions* Aelian
120   *and at last, seers* Clement of Alexandria Plutarch
120   *Strife accursed* Plutarch
120   *and tenacious* Simplicius
121   *Now listen: how* Simplicius
121   *They are one* Hippolytus
121   *By Love's love* Sextus Empiricus

122   *a boy, a girl* Diogenes Laertius
122   *Narrow is the cunning* Pseudo-Aristotle
122   *The drugs that cure* Plutarch
123   *But what idiots* Plutarch & Hippolytus
123   *No wise man* Porphyry
123   *It is proclaimed* Scholia on Nicander's *Theriaca*
124   *For god they didn't* Porphyry
124   *If only I had died* Sextus Empiricus
124   *A father will* Sextus Empiricus
125   *and will not cease* Clement of Alexandria
125   *And so, angered* Clement of Alexandria
125   *weeping and wailing* Hierocles
125   *a joyless place* Porphyry
125   *arrived underneath* Plutarch
125   *all-covering earth* Clement of Alexandria
126   *Blessed, who gains* Clement of Alexandria
126   *No human head* Ammonius
126   *For humans* Aristotle
126   *As far as they grow* Aristotle
126   *As when painters* Simplicius
127   *As when, mind* Aristotle
127   *No easy task* Clement of Alexandria
127   *If you place* Hippolytus
128   *The heart, nurtured* Stobaeus

Acknowledgments

Thank you to the editors of the journals that published portions of this book: *Reliquiae* for Anaximenes and an excerpt of Parmenides, *Ancient Exchanges* for Xenophanes, and *Poetry* for a section of Empedocles. Thank you to Daniela Cascella for including a suite of translations in *MAP*, and to Kylan Rice for responding to those with a poem of his own.

& largest thanks to Martin Corless-Smith, whose *Free Poetry* has championed this project and whose generosity has made a new nest for ancient song.

& something larger even than thanks, some gratitude I don't know the word for, to Daniel Slager and all those at Milkweed Editions. To be given a home—

DAN BEACHY-QUICK is the translator of *Stone-Garland*, as well as the author of two works of creative nonfiction, *Of Song and Silence* and *The Whaler's Dictionary*, nine collections of poems, one novel, and a monograph on the work of John Keats. His work has been a winner of the Colorado Book Award, a finalist for the William Carlos Williams Prize and the PEN/USA Literary Award in Poetry, longlisted for the National Book Award for Poetry, and included in the *Best American Poetry* anthology. The recipient of a Lannan Foundation residency, his work has been supported by the Woodberry Poetry Room at Harvard University and the Guggenheim Foundation. He is a University Distinguished Teaching Scholar at Colorado State University, where he serves in the English department and teaches in the MFA program in creative writing.

ABOUT SEEDBANK

Just as repositories around the world gather seeds in an effort
to ensure biodiversity in the future, Seedbank gathers works
of literature from around the world that foster reflection on
the relationship of human beings with place and
the natural world.

SEEDBANK FOUNDERS

The generous support of the following visionary investors

makes this series possible:

Meg Anderson and David Washburn

Anonymous

The Hlavka Family

milkweed
EDITIONS

Founded as a nonprofit organization in 1980, Milkweed Editions is an independent publisher. Our mission is to identify, nurture, and publish transformative literature, and build an engaged community around it.

Milkweed Editions is based in Bdé Óta Othúŋwe (Minneapolis) within Mní Sota Makhóčhe, the traditional homeland of the Dakhóta people. Residing here since time immemorial, Dakhóta people still call Mní Sota Makhóčhe home, with four federally recognized Dakhóta nations and many more Dakhóta people residing in what is now the state of Minnesota. Due to continued legacies of colonization, genocide, and forced removal, generations of Dakhóta people remain disenfranchised from their traditional homeland. Presently, Mní Sota Makhóčhe has become a refuge and home for many Indigenous nations and peoples, including seven federally recognized Ojibwe nations. We humbly encourage our readers to reflect upon the historical legacies held in the lands they occupy.

milkweed.org

Milkweed Editions, an independent nonprofit publisher, gratefully acknowledges sustaining support from our Board of Directors; the Alan B. Slifka Foundation and its president, Riva Ariella Ritvo-Slifka; the Amazon Literary Partnership; the Ballard Spahr Foundation; *Copper Nickel*; the McKnight Foundation; the National Endowment for the Arts; the National Poetry Series; and other generous contributions from foundations, corporations, and individuals. Also, this activity is made possible by the voters of Minnesota through a Minnesota State Arts Board Operating Support grant, thanks to a legislative appropriation from the arts and cultural heritage fund. For a full listing of Milkweed Editions supporters, please visit milkweed.org.

Interior design by Tijqua Daiker and Mary Austin Speaker
Typeset in Caslon

Adobe Caslon Pro was created by Carol Twombly
for Adobe Systems in 1990. Her design was inspired by
the family of typefaces cut by the celebrated engraver
William Caslon I, whose family foundry served
England with clean, elegant type from the early
Enlightenment through the turn of the
twentieth century.